STRATEGY & TACTICS OF SEA WARFARE

Marshall Cavendish London & New York

Edited by **Will Fowler**

Published by
Marshall Cavendish Books Limited
58 Old Compton Street
London W1V 5PA

© Marshall Cavendish Limited 1979
This volume first published 1979

Printed in Great Britain

ISBN 0 85685 505 7

Published by
Marshall Cavendish Books Limited

CONTENTS

PICTURE LIST
Armada de Chile 10/11
Bettman Archive 8
Camera Press 13TL & C
COI 66/7
Mark Dartford/Robert Paulley 16, 18/9, 23
KW Grutzemacher 24, 39T
W Fowler 30/1
Michael Holford 5
Foto Druppel 38
Keystone 63
J G Moore Collection 13 TR
Imperial War Museum 4C, 15, 25, 26, 27, 32, 33, 35, 40, 44,
45, 53
McDonnell Aircraft Corporation 64
Ministry of Defence 65, 68/9, 70/1, 72/3, 76/7
MOD/Eric North 41
MOD/JG Moore Collection 60/1, 74/5, 78/9, 80
US Navy 4T, 42, 54/5
US Navy/JG Moore Collection 48/9, 56/7, 59
USSR Navy 79
Wiener 39C

ARTWORKS
Creative Cartography/Nick Skelton 50/1
Sarson & Bryan 9
Ray Woodward/Blamdford Press Ltd 6, 7

Sea Power and its development until 1914

Sea power is the means by which a nation, or a group of nations acting together, attempts to secure and maintain command of the sea so that it can transport its own mercantile and military resources necessary for the prosecution of a war effort. In doing so it naturally attempts to deny such facilities to the enemy. The strategic elements involved in maintaining this power range from building up shipbuilding and ordnance facilities, bases in the homeland and abroad, fishing, mercantile and hydrographic fleets, to the final arbiter of sea power, the fighting ship. On the latter ultimately depends the safe passage of the other ships and the security of the homeland.

Warships are compromise constructions in that they combine defensive protection, propulsion and endurance facilities with offensive power. This has been true throughout history, thus the nature and power of a fighting ship at any given time is dependent on the level of technology at that time. Warships, at least, have always tended to be built around the most powerful weapon in existence, or in support of the ship that carries that weapon. In the present century, however, technology has produced both weapons and means of delivery that have vied with one another to be the decisive weapon at sea; and these weapons have produced specialization of ships and altered strategic and tactical concepts concerning their employment.

At the time of the French Revolutionary and Napoleonic Wars there was only one type of naval vessel: the wooden fighting ship, built around a crude, inaccurate, short-range cannon. The destructive power of such cannons was so small that they needed to be mounted in broadsides and to be used at very short ranges to be of any use at all. This had two effects. Firstly, it meant that the gun decks had to be heavy enough to take the weight of many guns and the sides had to be strong enough to afford some degree of protection for the gun crews. The weights implied in such considerations meant that the ships had to rely on wind and tide for movement since independent movement by means of oars was out of the question. Secondly, in the field of tactics, the nature of the ship determined that it had to fight in broadside action since it lacked any means of forward or rear offensive power (or any substance). This meant that a force seeking action had to secure the advantage of wind conditions in order to bring an enemy to bay. If an enemy was inferior but had the better of the weather conditions there was very little a superior enemy could do to force action since he

had no superiority in speed with which to close the range. The sailing ships of all nations were roughly the same (hence the rough equality of speed), since the prevailing level of technology – knowledge of ship-building techniques, skill in sail and rope making, the forging of cannon and shot – was roughly the same in Europe and North America. It was continually evolving and advancing (albeit very slowly), yet in essence the ships of the latter sixteenth, seventeenth, eighteenth and early nineteenth centuries were similar in construction, performance, skill of crews and in their dependence on the elements for movement.

The purpose of sea power was primarily defensive. The over-riding aim was the defence of the integrity of the homeland against invasion and raids against which military forces would otherwise have to be deployed. In the case of Britain, an island kingdom off the coast of a Europe littered with states that possessed armies larger than her own, this was the whole of the *raison d'etre* of the navy: other countries, being continental, needed navies for exactly the same reason but were not so absolutely dependent on sea power for national survival as the British. In the search for security against naval attack certain strategic interests could be of immense importance (for instance, for Britain the prevention of the Low Countries being occupied by a hostile major power because of the proximity of those areas to the east coast of England), the normal tactic employed was the close blockade of enemy ports by an equal or superior fleet. In the era of the sailing ship such a policy was always possible for the British because such ships had immense endurance – as long as discipline and fresh water lasted – and did not have to return to port for refuelling. Moreover, if winds drove the British from their stations (off the French and/or Spanish ports since these were Britain's natural enemies) those same south-westerly winds confined the enemy to their ports. In addition, the British were more favoured with suitable ports than were the French and Spanish on their Atlantic coastlines. Geography and meteorology therefore conferred on Britain immense benefits in naval warfare with her normal enemies in the days of sailing ships. It was to do so again in the changed circumstances of the twentieth century in the struggle to realize the second objective of sea power – the defence of trade.

A glance at a world map of 1914 quickly reveals the two most salient features of the British Empire, namely its immensity and its essentially maritime nature.

Largely, but by no means wholly, built up in the era of the sailing ship, the British Empire had been acquired by sea power. Nearly every point of constriction was held by Britain, virtually every point where communications were forced through a narrow sea passage was held by the British; every point where narrowness of sea passage had marked out a battlefield for the great powers was controlled by the Royal Navy. Wind and currents had determined the location of these positions in the days of sailing ships, coal bunkers in the age of steam. By 1914, by dint of efforts in past wars, Gibraltar, Malta, Port Said, Suez, Aden, the Persian Gulf, Colombo, Singapore, Hong Kong, Mombasa, Cape Town, Freetown, the Falklands, the West Indies, New Zealand – all were under the British flag. From these positions, and from her home ports, Britain controlled the major part of the world's trade; from these positions she could immediately bring pressure to bear

against any other country; in these places could be assembled the means of protecting merchant ships – the convoy system of merchantmen sailing together under armed escort provided by the Royal Navy.

Thus the functions of sea power were essentially twofold in their historic evolution: the security against invasion and the defence of trade. In the days before railways and motor transport, these were of immense importance, proportionately even more so than they are today. The reverse of these functions, however, was also of great importance: command of the seas allowed the holder to pick the time and place for an invasion, expedition or raid that formed part of his intention to make an enemy conform to his will; command of the seas also allowed the commerce of an eneny to be seized; *lack* of command of the seas (on the latter point) was an encouragement to a country to furnish commerce raiders to seek out lone enemy merchantmen in order to bring supplies to home ports.

There remained two further functions of sea power, applicable in times of peace and war. Firstly, the existence of a fleet intact was a powerful instrument of diplomacy, a bargaining chip at the conference table, the means of extracting concessions, of reaching accommodations that would be beyond recall if the fleet did not exist. In time of war such a fleet could also tie down the resources of an enemy that were urgently needed for such operations as a colonial expedition or defence against commerce raiders. Secondly, fighting ships could 'show the flag,' as an instrument of diplomacy, a symbol of power, intent and capability: in the nineteenth century this was a role virtually synonymous with the Royal Navy.

The ships that carried out these functions, as noted earlier, were of a single nature – wooden sailing ships with broadsides of cannons. These ships divided into two basic types: the line of battle ship and the frigate; the basic distinction being in the number of gun decks carried. A line of battle ship was, by definition, a ship that could take its place in a battle line against the heaviest enemy ships; such ships carried upwards of three gun decks. Frigates, much nimbler but not necessarily faster, usually carried a single deck of guns and were used as scouts, message carriers and commerce protection. In carrying out their appointed roles both were hampered by problems of communication – gun smoke, rigging and light winds made visual signalling difficult, and admirals had many problems in controlling their fleets once in action. It was also hard to take advantage of sudden opportunities that arose in the course of a conflict. Overall this had the effect of stifling initiative, since the simplest solution was to adopt a line ahead formation in action, ships taking on their opposite numbers in the enemy line. Such theories were first laid down in England in 1653 as *Fighting Instructions* and elaborated later in 1673. These became, with some modifications, holy writ for the Royal Navy in the seventeenth and eighteenth centuries. Admirals could depart from the line of battle formation only at their peril and there was no encouragement to break the enemy line in order to provoke a melee or secure an annihilating advantage over part of the enemy fleet. Only in the case of an enemy in flight could the sanctity of the battle line be broken in the General Chase. Blind adherence to these ideas frequently resulted in indecisive battles, and Professor Lewis in *The History of the British Navy* has pointed

out that between 1692 and 1782 fifteen orthodox 'line' battles resulted in not one enemy ship being sunk or captured, whereas six 'chases' resulted in overwhelming British victories. The tactical sterility of the line tactics, which caused battles to be decided by geographical position and strategic deployment rather than initiative, did result in improved signalling techniques being introduced by Howe and Kampenfelt, but eventually the whole concept was challenged theoretically by writers such as de Morogues, Clerk and de Grenier and practically by admirals such as Nelson. It remains a fact, however, that no matter how frequently the line tactics showed their futility in war, they were always reimposed in peace time. This was certainly the case after the Napoleonic Wars, but there was one very important development at this time which almost guaranteed change: the Industrial Revolution in its application to sea warfare.

In the fifty years after Trafalgar the homogenity of ship design that had been carefully evolved over the previous two hundred years disintegrated under the impact of a rapidly advancing technology in which there were no guide lines and no pools of accumulated knowledge on which to draw. Ships underwent profound change. Independent movement was restored by the introduction of first paddle and then screw propul-

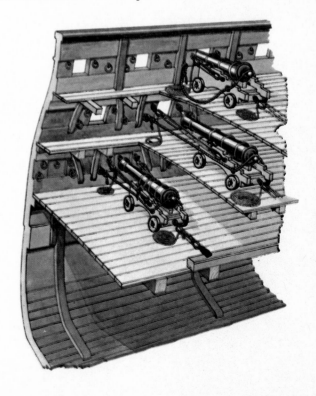

7

sion; guns became heavier, rifled and fired shells. The new shells necessitated protection other than wood and led initially to ships being sheathed wholly or in part by iron and then to ships made entirely of iron. Broadsides were suppressed as were sails and masts. Guns began to be mounted on revolving turntables to enable them to be trained over wide arcs of fire, and they were enclosed by turrets to protect the crews. By 1870 the ships of different navies varied vastly in design, capability and sea worthiness.

Moreover, not only were ships being changed by the evolution of gunnery but, under the impact of metallurgical and chemical developments, new weapons were emerging as potential rivals to the gun. These weapons aimed at striking an enemy ship at its most vulnerable point below the water line. The search for such weapons (other than the ram) can be traced back over three centuries but it was not until the nineteenth that technology enabled them to be developed. The

first of the new weapons was the mine (initially called the torpedo), and its invention is generally credited to Samuel Colt, although work on such a weapon was taking place in various places at the same time. Colt invented a mine – a metal-enclosed explosive charge – that could be detonated by electric current operated from an observation post on land. Subsequently, contact mines were developed that exploded when in collision with a ship. Early mines were naturally primitive but the passage of time permitted more effective explosives to be used, more efficient initiation to be adopted and the development of a reliable method of laying mines at a proscribed depth. (The latter was achieved by laying mines from a specialized craft with an attached anchor, cable and hydrostat that fixed the mine at the required depth.)

Mines had immense strategic and tactical effects. They were used extensively during the Crimean war (1854–56) but caused no losses (the first ship to be lost to mines was the *USS Cairo* in 1862, in the Battle of the Yazoo River). Thereafter their increasing effectiveness meant that a policy of close blockade of an enemy coast became increasingly unrealistic, for mines, a cheap mass produced weapon needing no maintenance and little manpower to use, were ideal defensive weapons for coastal and harbour protection, denying the room to manoeuvre for an aggressive fleet. Offensively, moreover, the mine could be used to try to restrict an enemy in his harbours.

The second of the new weapons was the 'locomotive torpedo' – an underwater weapon with its own means of propulsion which differentiated it from other forms of torpedoes that demanded death wishes on the part of their users. (The *USS Housatonic*, in 1864, was the first major surface ship to be sunk by underwater attack when a Confederate hand-cranked submarine detonated a charge under her: the submarine perished in the attempt, such were the dangers of early types of torpedo.) The 'locomotive torpedo' was pioneered by an Austrian, Luppis, and a Scot, Whitehead, in Fiume. It was erratic in its direction and depth-keeping capabilities, but could only improve. After the late seventies contra-rotating propellers, the horizontal rudder and the gyroscope conspired together to enhance its potency; by the 1890s a torpedo with a 300-lb warhead had a 1000 yard range at 30 knots (or 4000 yards at 19 knots) and could be fired from below the waterline of a moving ship.

The development of such a weapon had to have

A German naval mine. 1 Glass tube containing a bichromate solution. If the glass was broken the solution met a zinc carbon plate. 2 Electric current ran through a fuse wire to a detonator. 3 Firing the main charge 4. The mine was secured by a cable which was anchored to a weight that rested on the sea bed.

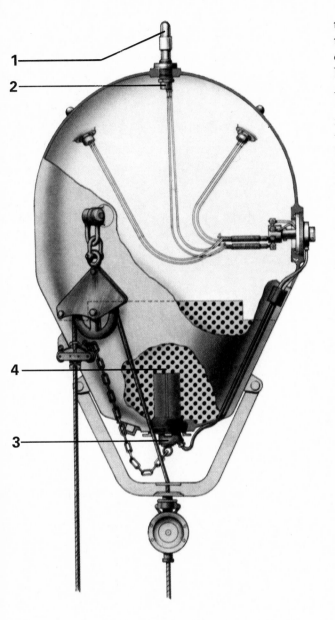

they could be used offensively, even with the primitive torpedoes then available. Nevertheless, the restrictions on the use of such craft could only be overcome by building larger and faster craft. The British built the *Lightning*, so named because of her 19 knots speed capacity. By the turn of the century torpedo boats were rising in displacement, speed and armament, and there was a need for a ship that could take on such boats before they could get into a position to attack the battle line. The British, since they had a strong battle fleet, tended to build 'destroyers' with a good turn of speed and quite heavy gun armaments: many other navies, especially the German Navy, tended to build smaller but faster boats with stronger torpedo armament since they were more interested in the offensive than defensive possibilities.

The second means of delivering torpedo attack was the submarine, developed around the turn of the century. The previously insurmountable problems encountered in building submarines had been overcome by technology. Steel provided a suitable material for construction; the horizontal rudder (hopefully) controlled the dive; and the internal combustion engine and accumulator battery provide a safe and reliable means of propulsion. By 1900 six navies had ten submarines among them, the British, alert to the danger that this vessel could be to their naval supremacy, quickly taking the lead in this field. It was the British who incorporated the conning tower and periscope into the first prototype submarines and led the field in submarine development up until the outbreak of World War I.

The third method of torpedo delivery was from the air, and the first occasion that this was achieved was one week before the outbreak of World War I. It had no immediate strategic or tactical impact, but air power was beginning to make itself felt in small ways on naval thinking before World War I though it was the war itself that gave this new dimension of warfare its main impetus.

The torpedo had one decisive effect on tactical thinking: it forced ranges to open. In the course of the nineteenth century, there was little real appreciation of how battles would be fought and the Nelsonian dictum that a captain could do no wrong if he placed his ship alongside the enemy was still widely held to be applicable. The advent of heavy guns in the sixties and seventies did nothing to change this because their accuracy rate was very low. [In one test in 1871 a

immense repercussions on naval warfare for, by its very existence, it required a new means of delivery and a revision of tactics. Over the years three ways of delivery were developed.

Initially, as early as 1870, special 'torpedo boats' were built but these were small, not particularly seaworthy and lacked range and crew accommodation. Primarily they were intended to be used for harbour defence although, as the Russians showed when two of their craft sank a Turkish guardship at Batum in 1878,

Huascar, an ironclad monitor built by the British for the Peruvians in 1865. She was powered by sail or steam and had a powerful twin 10-in gun turret and armour protection with a robust ram bow.

British battleship, at 200 yards, missed another battleship target, both ships being anchored; in the Spanish-American war of 1898 the Americans had to close to under 300 yards against moored opponents in order to achieve hits and then only scored 3 per cent accuracy rate (Manila Bay).] The torpedo, however, forced these ranges to open because battleships dared not get so close in case they were exposed to underwater attack. Torpedoes also forced the heavier ships to carry secondary and tertiary armament to deal with torpedo boats before they came within effective range. Mixed

armament of heavy, medium and light guns was therefore needed for a battleship in order to fight heavy ships and defend itself against torpedo attacks. Mixed armament was also considered necessary to provide the heavy volume of fire that was held to be the key to victory, in part a reaction against the monster guns of earlier decades that were slow to handle and low in accuracy. The development of quick-firing guns in the eighties enabled a heavy volume of fire to be put down by a ship, but the increasing range at which actions had to be fought to keep out of the range of torpedoes

Strategically and tactically the *Dreadnought* had a profound effect. Strategically, she was so superior to previous types of battleship in her firepower and speed that she inaugurated a naval race between the powers for superiority in numbers of this type of ship. This eventually became an Anglo-German race, won ultimately by the British but only at a profound cost in relations between the two countries. Tactically, in opening the range of action and demanding accurate gunnery at high speed, the *Dreadnought* required a fresh tactical approach to her handling. The acquisition of more gun power and greater speed could only be an advantage if used to secure an overwhelming concentration of force; but in fact the tactical deployment of most navies remained the line ahead formation, with the battle line being manoeuvred as a single inflexible whole. The aim of such deployment was to secure the most favourable conditions – wind clearing gun and funnel smoke, light and sun – for concentration against the enemy line, ideally with the broadside of the line being concentrated against the enemy vanguard. This was known as 'Crossing the T.' Much thought went into considering ways to ensure the timely deployment of the battleships from their cruising formation – a compact mass covered by attendant craft – into a battle line where the fullest possible weight of fire power could be brought to bear on an enemy. Less thought went into the manner in which the squadrons that made up the fleet could be used in a semi-independent role, thereby encouraging initiative and aggression. Great emphasis was placed on conformity and wooden orthodoxy, with too great a reliance being placed on the commander of the fleet to see, know and order everything.

The problems of the fleet commander were greatly increased by the new developments. He still had to contend with old problems such as smoke, which often made flag signalling impossible (although he was aided by the introduction of radio before the war), but the battlefield had been extended by the restoration of independent movement and any battle was bound to be a fast moving affair. There was an increasing need to know the location and strength of the enemy at all times through detailed reconnaissance and reporting. This was the role of the cruiser. Cruisers had been eclipsed by iron battleships against which they could neither fight nor run away since they lacked metal construction or any superiority in speed. The first iron cruiser was the British *Inconstant*, almost as large as

meant that fire control became increasingly difficult. Different calibre guns and shells meant different flight times of shells to a given range and difficulty in identifying individual fall of shot. In the early twentieth century the principle of centralized fire control was established and with it uniformity of guns, which allowed the accurate firing of salvoes as long as the guns were of the same size. The first ship to incorporate a uniform heavy armament was *HMS Dreadnought* (launched 1906) though the Americans had been the first to announce their intention of building such a ship.

contemporary battleships. There was a temptation for second class naval powers to use heavily protected cruisers in a dual role as cruisers and line ships, but in fact theoretical and metallurgical developments led to a diversification of cruiser evolution into two main themes. On the one hand, the French development of the *Guerre de Course* strategy of commerce raiding by surface ships led to the evolution of heavy cruisers, fast enough to evade battleships but capable of looking after themselves by virtue of their strong gun armament. The French initiated this process with the *Dupuy de Lome* in 1888, a 20-knot ship which made her a little slow in comparison with contemporary cruisers, but armed with 7.6-in and 6.4-in guns. There followed a race between the British and French in heavy cruisers, in which the example of the *Inconstant* was virtually repeated by the *Powerful* and *Terrible* in that they were almost as large and costly as line ships. The development of steel made for better quality cruisers on lower displacements, but even in the first decade of the present century there was a tendency for size, speed, protection and armament to increase again. The culmination of the process was to be seen in the battle-cruisers, initiated by the British at the time of the *Dreadnought*. Almost as large as the *Dreadnought*, they were nearly as powerful in main armament, and much faster, than contemporary battleships. Battlecruisers were specifically designed for the twin purposes of hunting down and destroying commerce raiders and acting as the fast vanguard of the battle fleet, capable of carrying out unaided a reconnaissance in force and of lying in the battle line. The weakness of the battle-cruiser concept, certainly in the British case though less so in the German and Japanese Navies, was that the tactical advantage of high speed – being able to choose range and position in an exchange of fire – was bought at too high a price in defensive power: the battle-cruisers could not take the punishment they themselves could inflict.

The light cruiser, on the other hand, was not intended to take punishment. Its task was to make contact with the enemy and to retain it until fleet contact was obtained: the light cruiser was in other words, the eyes of the fleet. Once battle was joined the reconnaissance role remained, but the light cruisers were supposed to afford protection to the battle line from enemy cruiser and destroyer attacks with torpedoes, and to launch such actions themselves. For the British before 1914 the defensive aspect of this role was the more important.

The destroyers in the Royal Navy had priorities that were essentially defensive though they were exceptional in that they were allocated an offensive role for night operations. On the whole, the Navy tried to avoid night action on the grounds that it was something of a lottery, but while the battle line would decline night action, the destroyers were given the initiative to launch attacks on the enemy line that would be perilous if mounted in daylight. Destroyers were generally exercised before the war in co-operation with the battle line by both the British and the Germans. Both Navies realized that co-ordination of gun and torpedo attacks was more likely to bring results than separate efforts: equally both Navies based their tactics not on individual ship attack but on flotilla attacks, in the belief that the concentration given by a flotilla of destroyers would be harder to avoid. The tactical response of the battle line to such attack was generally agreed to be 'the turn away from the attack' – exposure on a small stern with its disturbed wake of water that was moving away from the torpedo. In this way the battle line could outrun the torpedoes as the latter began to slow down when they approached the end of their runs. This tactic was preferred to the ploy of turning towards the torpedoes and 'combing' them which was considered dangerous because the converging speeds of ship and weapon made evasive action more difficult. The weakness of the safer turn away was that the ship ran the risk of losing contact with the enemy battle line.

Destroyers also carried out an anti-submarine role in forming a screen for the heavy ships when the latter were either in their cruising or their battle formation. The effectiveness of destroyers in such a role was very limited before 1916 since they lacked the means of detecting or attacking a submerged craft other than gunfire or ramming. Despite these limitations, however, they were effective in keeping submarines away from the fleet: indeed between 1914 and 1916 only one instance of the British destroyer screen being penetrated by a German submarine was reported – and that resulted in the ramming of the submarine in question by the *Dreadnought*. Nevertheless, the threat of submarines imposed certain quite severe restrictions on the strategic and tactical handling of battle formations. Strategically, fleets did not dare to enter certain waters: in order to move at all they had to employ continual high speed cruising formation and often zig-zag – all the time cutting down the range of the destroyers, and hence the fleet itself. Submarines themselves could be

used in defence of approaches to ports and coasts – but this was generally recognized to be a weak arrangement that was costly in manpower and resources and not likely to achieve very much. More emphasis was placed on their offensive use, either individually or in an extended line, for both reconnaissance or opportunity attacks on the enemy battle formation. Tactically, in battle an enemy fleet could be drawn across a patrol line into a submarine 'killing zone,' and for this reason the British were somewhat reluctant to follow an enemy that 'stood off' during an engagement. The tactic was more theoretical than real, however, since the low speeds of submarines, both on the surface and while submerged, made close co-ordination very difficult indeed though the threat was real and remained. In these roles the submarine was seen basically as an adjunct to the big gun, rather than as a weapon with an

independent role to play, and before 1914 only a very few people considered the possibility that its chief role could be that of commerce destruction. Since a submarine could not take off crews of merchantmen, it was not seriously entertained that any civilized nation could resort to such an operation since it would involve either killing or setting adrift defenceless merchant sailors.

To summarize the situation prior to 1914 is difficult because of the many different strands involved. Material and tactics were dominated by the big gun and its use in broadside on an extended battle line. The battleship was no longer the absolute ruler of the seas but was under challenge, though the First World War was to show that that challenge was for the moment over-rated. Fear of the new weapons, however, bred caution both in the strategic employment of fleets and tactical handling at sea.

The First World War, triumph of Sea Power

Stores and munitions burn in Anzac Town as the guns
of H.M.S. *Cornwallis* cover the Allied withdrawal from
Gallipoli.

Before the war a French general made the celebrated remark that the British Navy was not worth a single bayonet. Though he was speaking the truth in that he was concerned with an initial clash of arms on the land frontiers, he failed to recognize the extent to which the capacity of France and Britain to wage war at all rested on sea power and the decisive part it could play in any war not decided in the opening exchanges. Had the Anglo-French armies been crushed in the opening battles – as they were in 1940 – there would have been very little the navies could have done to retrieve the situation: that the armies were not defeated but could not, in their turn, impose their will on the enemy ensured that sea power played an absolutely vital, indeed crucial, part in the Allied victory. It was a role that was unglamourous, even insidious, but it was sea power that ultimately strangled the life and will out of the Central Powers. Official sources placed the number of German civilian deaths between 1914 and 1918 as a direct result of blockade as high as 800,000; certainly it was despair at the prospects of having to endure the

Close up of a British dreadnought's 12in
gun turrets with 12pdr quick-firers on top. A feature
of many dreadnought battleships was a turret or two
mounted amidships near the centre line to obtain
maximum firepower.
The 20,000-ton dreadnought HMS
Hercules with her ten 12in guns traversed to port
during the Battle of Jutland. Primitive fire-control,
smoke and darkness frustrated a battlefleet with
unsurpassed gunpower.

winter of 1918-19 after the disasters of the previous one, that played a large part in the German collapse in the autumn of 1918.

In World War I the Allies possessed certain basic advantages over the Central Powers, foremost among them their considerable superiority in numbers of ships of all types, and a well-nigh absolute superiority in geographical position. Through her metropolitan and imperial positions, Britain sat astride the trade routes of

the Central Powers in both the Mediterranean and the Atlantic and was thus in a position to sever virtually all her enemies' trade, with the notable and vital exception of German trade with Sweden.

The British policy of blockade was implemented by three measures: the basing of the fleet in the north of Scotland, the patrolling of the seas between Scotland and Greenland and Scotland and Norway, and the mining and patrolling of the English Channel. The Channel was mined, with gaps left for shipping only between the Kent coast and the Goodwin Sands, thus making it a very easy task for the British to intercept any merchantman passing through the Straits of Dover. In the north the British started the war with eight vintage cruisers, well enough armed to deal with any likely opponent, to patrol the routes to Germany: after November 1914 requisitioned liners were used as armed merchant cruisers to patrol these waters. The latter ships had the great advantage over military cruisers of good turns of speed when necessary and very long endurance: indeed the flagship, the *Alsatian*, once cruised at thirteen knots for forty days on patrol.

The northern partrol operated search lines with ships ten miles apart, south of the Shetlands and west of Norway in the early stages of the war but gradually evolving ever more complicated patrol patterns that proved remarkably effective in preventing the blockade from being breached. Such patrols could not be 100 per cent effective since night and poor visibility always gave a blockade runner a chance of getting through, but the success of the measures can be gauged from the fact that between December 1914 and June 1915 over 1610 ships were investigated and nearly 400 were detained for further search. In the whole of 1916 over 3000 ships were investigated.

Such a policy was bound to conflict with neutral interests since the shipping trade was very lucrative. If a ship was detained for search the British could seize her if she was carrying war materiel, such as guns or explosives, or if certain goods, such as foodstuffs or raw materials, could be shown to be destined for the armed forces or government of the enemy. Certain

goods, including raw cotton, oil and rubber, were immune under the terms of the 1909 Declaration of London (never ratified by the British). By the beginning of 1915, as the realization dawned that the war might be a long one, the British began to declare certain items that were 'free' or 'conditional contraband' as 'absolute contraband.' They also began to enforce their measures more severely, although this raised problems with countries such as the Netherlands and the USA. It was not until the Americans entered the War in 1917 that the Allies were able to ignore those rights that the US had championed when uninvolved. In the meantime, however, the British had resorted to various ploys to avoid friction with neutral countries: in August 1915, they declared cotton as absolute contraband with no American protest because they had already bought virtually the whole of the American cotton crop; they made bilateral arrangements with the Norwegians, Danes and Dutch (September 1) in order to ensure that those countries did not supply Germany with goods that the British let through to them. They also resorted to the purchase of entire ships' cargoes (above the market value) simply to prevent trouble. By such measures, the British were able to draw the teeth of neutral opposition and to add vehemence to the blockade. After July 1917, the Allies added various foodstuffs and forage to the conditional contraband list, and to the absolute or conditional lists virtually all types of vegetable, animal and natural oil, virtually every significant ore, mineral and chemical, most forms of yarn, and a whole list of industrial materials and equipment. In all 238 items (excluding derivatives and by-products) were on the banned lists. The effect was devastating. As early as 1915, German harvest yields began to fall as a result of the demands for explosives and the lack of nitrate imports. By 1918, cereal production had fallen 40 per cent from its 1912-13 level; potato production by nearly 50 per cent; sugar by 33 per cent. The situation for Germany's allies was even worse. It was not in the armies in the field but in the nation as a whole that the collapse occurred. This was in large part the result of the superiority of Allied seapower.

The policy of blockade from Dover and northern Scotland was one that had been decided upon during May 1912, when the close blockade of the German Bight had been abandoned in British war plans because of the danger from submarines and mines. Only as late as that had Britain adopted the policy of distant blockade, and even then she thought in terms of an observational blockade stretched across the North Sea. Early losses in 1914 forced her to discard an observation line, albeit reluctantly, for this smacked of a defensive mentality that was anathema to many naval officers. The redeeming feature (to the British Navy) of blockade was that its rigours might force the German Navy to come out and fight: the Royal Navy overall was convinced that the German fleet would go the way of previous enemies. Overwhelming decisive victory was what the British public demanded; it was also what the world expected. Here was a major problem for the Admiralty and the Commander-in-Chief of the Grand Fleet, Jellicoe, who had no illusions about the reality of the situation. Jellicoe clearly appreciated that Britain did not have to fight to retain command of the seas: she was in the position that she merely had to avoid defeat in order to keep Germany at bay in a position of inferiority. He also realized, on the other hand, that a naval defeat would have incalculable results – perhaps catastrophic ones among the neutrals – and would leave open to attack the whole of Anglo-French trade upon which depended the survival of the Allies. Such were Jellicoe's strategic considerations. His tactical deliberations were similarly defensive and, being defensive, Jellicoe partially forfeited the likelihood of decisive engagement, since an inferior German fleet was more likely to try to avoid action than accept it.

Jellicoe wanted to bring the Germans to battle under circumstances most favourable to the British. Therefore, in his tactical deliberations he had to consider that, in addition to being limited to a range of 900 miles from his bases (because of the limited endurance of the fleet escorts), he had to avoid an action in the southern North Sea where the threat of mines and torpedoes was at its greatest. Because of this threat Jellicoe made it clear that he intended not to comply with an enemy turnaway when in contact since this could be an attempt to draw the British fleet into a submarine or mine trap. Thus two major strategic decisions – the geographical advantage of the British Isles *vis-a-vis* Germany and the need to avoid defeat – fortified the existing fear of new and largely untried weapons and fatally restricted aggressive tactical deployment.

For the Germans the situation was very different. They had built their navy following the 1898 and 1900 Navy Laws with the deliberate intention of exacting

Friedrich der Grosse **a Kaiser Class battleship probably at her surrender in 1918. Coal burning ships produced funnel smoke which could be a liability in action. During the Battle of the Dogger Bank, the British had hoped to secure a position to the east which would have cut off the Germans from the home ports and given the Royal Navy the advantage of the light and a breeze to clear the funnel smoke away.**

concessions from the British: this had merely resulted in estranged Anglo-German relations. Now, in time of war, the Navy was powerless to prevent German trade disappearing from the surface of the oceans with no corresponding gains for the Germans outside Europe. The German Pacific Squadron was effectively written off with the outbreak of war; although the imaginative and aggressive handling of this squadron led, in fact, to its having a longer life and a more useful one than might otherwise have been the case. Nevertheless, if the German Navy was very inactive in the first months of the war in the defence of German overseas interests and trade, it did play a vitally important role throughout the war simply as 'a fleet in being' which, undefeated, prevented the dispersal of the enemy battle fleet and light forces for other urgent tasks. Since the British needed to concentrate all their available strength in the North Sea, for it was up to the Germans when, if and in what strength to make a move, the Royal Navy could not allocate much of its strength to secondary theatres. The full effect of sea power could therefore never be fully brought to bear as long as the German fleet remained intact. Moreover, for the Germans the battle fleet existed as a line of defence for limited tactical mobility for light surface ships and as distant support for commerce raiders. As long as the High Sea Fleet remained intact, British minesweepers and minelayers could not move into the German Bight in an effort to confine the Germans to their harbours. If they did the German light forces would have countered them, and any escalation of the scale of action would have resulted in the British battle line being engaged in the southern North Sea very close to Germany and far from its own bases. The Grand Fleet could only afford to take losses in the German Bight if the German battle fleet was already sunk; as long as it remained there was no way that the British could risk a deep penetration in the North Sea. This being so the commerce raiders were left with room to get to sea. The German battle fleet, however, was not simply passive. It, like the Grand Fleet, sought battle but only on its terms and these terms included a preliminary equalization of strength by mine and torpedo warfare – which, in fact, never materialized. Unless the Germans could lessen the odds against them, or catch only part of the Grand Fleet, they were not prepared to seek a stand-up fight. Given this reluctance to stand and fight there was little the Royal Navy could do to force the issue. For the most part the

Germans were content to use their main fleets on small scale operations rather than on fleet actions against the British. Such operations included co-operation with the Army in the Baltic against the Russians and the militarily insignificant, but politically and morally beneficial, hit-and-run raids on the English east coast and operations in conjunction with the Army against the Russians in the Baltic.

The operations against the English east coast should have been reasonably safe affairs given the fact that the Grand Fleet base at Scapa Flow was so far away that the Germans might reasonably expect to be halfway home before the British were able to respond. This hope proved unreasonable for the Admiralty intelligence organization was very effective and, with the help of captured code books recovered by the Russians from the wrecked cruiser *Magdeburg*, was able to read German radio orders as rapidly as the intended recipients. Thus, when the Germans made a sortie with a main force of three battlecruisers and one armoured cruiser in January 1915 towards the Dogger Bank, with the intention of disrupting any British

fishing and naval units that might be in the area, the British were able to put five battlecruisers against them. (The Grand Fleet was in close support, though on this occasion it never came into action.) The subsequent action was very confused, with the light cruisers and destroyers, operating in the reconnaissance role, clashed on the flanks of the main forces. When the Germans realized that they had come into contact with a force considerably superior to themselves and that they had no possible support available, they attempted to flee to the south-east. The British would have preferred to have moved around the German rear to secure a position to the east of the Germans, where they would have had the advantage of the light, wind (to clear funnel smoke) and position between the German ships and their bases, but the fear of mines prevented their moving in that direction. The battle that followed was therefore a stern chase with the rear of the German line and the van of the British force taking fearful punishment as ranges closed. In the engagement, British tactical deployment was faulty in that the

slowest ship in line was left behind somewhat, thereby lessening the advantage of superiority of numbers, and British fire distribution went horribly astray. With the first two British ships correctly taking the German leading ship (though without accurate observation), the third and fourth British ships took on their opposite numbers, leaving the second German ship untouched. The first three German ships took on the British flagship which, heavily damaged, had to fall out of the line. In doing so, she issued a series of very confusing orders that led to the remaining four battleships breaking off the action and turning instead against the crippled armoured cruiser that had pulled out of the German line some fifteen minutes earlier. Poor signalling by flags (the radio had been shot away), a lack of initiative on the part of subordinates who unquestioningly followed orders in spite of the battle situation, poor gunnery and total confusion robbed the British of what should have been a considerable victory – though most of the lessons that could have been drawn from the battle were lost sight of in the euphoria.

The only fleet action of the war came briefly at Jutland (May 31/June 1 1916) when the pressure of blockade, the indecisive battles at Verdun and the need for the German Navy to do something to justify its existence and raise morale, led the Germans to seek an action that would result in the destruction of part of the Grand Fleet. From the start the Germans never intended to fight an extended action against a superior force, rather they hoped to make a 'demonstration' off the Norwegian or Danish coasts and hopefully lure part of the British forces on to their own battle line, acting in support of the demonstrating (battlecruiser) force. They also aimed to use submarines as reconnaissance forces and for opportunity attacks, in accordance with the strategy of whittling down British superiority of numbers. The British, informed by superb intelligence, were aware that some such operation was in the offing and similarly arranged their forces with the battlecruisers in the van and battle fleet in support. Overall the British deployed 28 battleships, 9 battlecruisers, 1 seaplane carrier and 112 cruisers and destroyers; the Germans had 16 battleships, 6 pre-dreadnought battleships, 5 battlecruisers and 72 cruisers and destroyers.

Initial contact was made between the cruisers of the battlecruiser forces at 2.20 p.m., the British battlecruisers turning south-south-east to engage the German battlecruisers as the latter turned to fall back on the German battle line. Because of a signals failure the British battlecruisers went into action with only a six to five advantage, because the four fast battleships in support failed to see their orders. Thus with more than half their gunfire unavailable in the opening exchange the British failed to make the most of their advantage, while the problem of the Dogger Bank, namely incorrect fire distribution, repeated itself. In what was known as 'The Run to the South' the British lost the *Indefatigable* and the *Queen Mary;* as the battleships, by cutting corners, came into line, however, an increasing toll was taken on the rear of the German line. The climax of this phase of the action came at 4.30 p.m. when, with the range closing, both sides launched massed destroyer attacks on the enemy line. As the destroyers clashed, both sides losing two ships, both of the battle lines turned away in accordance with tactical doctrine, and contact was temporarily lost. As both sides turned to renew contact the British light cruisers in the van of the force found the whole of the German battle line to their front. Their reports to the battlecruiser force enabled the British ships to turn

through sixteen points and reverse course in order to draw the Germans on to the Grand Fleet just as they had been drawn on to the German battle line. Because the British turned in succession through a given point rather than together, the last ships in the line (the battleships) took heavy punishment. But in 'The Run to the North' light conditions for once favoured the British and the German battlecruisers were further mauled to the extent that the van was forced to fall back and use torpedo attacks to relieve the pressure. In this melee the German cruisers were severely hammered by the timely intervention of more British battlecruisers acting as the van of the Grand Fleet. This intervention served to protect the deployment of the Grand Fleet into its battle formation, and to mask its presence from German scouting forces whose performance throughout the battle was unimpressive.

Though very badly served in a reconnaissance role by the battlecruisers, and severely handicapped by the inevitable navigational discrepancies, the final deployment of the Grand Fleet from its cruising to battle formation for the first phase of the battle fleet action was masterly, indeed seldom if ever surpassed. Moving east-south-east from the port column, the deployment ensured that the line crossed the German advance and wrapped around its side, thus securing the vital position between enemy and his base; it also enabled the British to have the very best of the deteriorating light, and prevented any masking of guns during the deployment. Moreover, any other movement could well have brought the line into range of torpedo attack while still not fully deployed. Though the Germans tried to fight back as they ran into a seemingly solid horizon of British battleships, the sheer weight of fire forced them to buckle since the van was bereft of most of its power because its batteries were masked.

To extricate themselves, the Germans carried out a sixteen-point turn, reversing the order of their line because the ships turned together, and carrying them away from the British line. This manoeuvre was carried out under cover of smoke and torpedo attack, and the skill with which it was carried out, combined with smoke and indifferent light, led to the British losing contact. Those ships that did see the manoeuvre did not report it to Jellicoe. The Grand Fleet did not immediately turn towards the enemy. Because of the approach of dusk – by this time it was about 6.42 p.m. – and the fear of torpedoes, the British concern was the maintenance of the fleet's strength and position

War and Commerce: Right: A convoy at the close of World War I; grouping ships only gave U-boats one opportunity for attack before they themselves were attacked. Below: The British High Seas Fleet in the North Sea.

between the enemy and his bases, for Jellicoe was confident of a resumption of action in the morning. The British steered south-west and then south *en echelon*, the divisions partially masking one another, when at about 7.10 p.m. they found themselves again crossing the German line. The Germans, having reversed their line by another sixteen-point turn together, tried to slip around the rear of the British line in the last of the light, but blundered into its centre. Once more the Germans came under merciless attack and they were forced to reverse order yet again under cover of smoke, and employ a torpedo attack and a suicidal lunge by the battlecruisers in order to draw fire. This time the British battle line had to turn away quite violently in order to outrun the torpedoes, and in doing so they lost contact and never regained it, though the battlecruisers did exchange fire between 8.23 and 8.40 p.m. – the last occasion in World War I when capital ships of the British and German Navies engaged one another.

With nightfall the tactical position changed: the British intended to decline action; the Germans were determined to break through to their bases at all costs since the alternative was to face annihilation the following morning. For the most part they were successful. The British destroyer screens placed behind the battle line to prevent such a breakthrough simply lacked the power to prevent the German thrust; the destroyers scored some successes but took very heavy losses in a one-sided action in which the Germans had the advantage of knowing the British night challenge. By the next morning the Germans were on the landward side of the Grand Fleet and safe. Overall neither side lost a battleship though the Germans lost a pre-dreadnought: the British lost three battlecruisers to the solitary German loss; three armoured cruisers to the four German light cruisers sunk and eight destroyers to the five German losses. Given the balance of naval forces the overall losses were roughly equal.

Tactically the battle was drawn, the Germans

UC-71, one of the submarines deployed by the Germans in World War I. She fought a savage four-hour battle with the 'Q' ship HMS *Dunraven* on August 8, 1917.

getting slightly the better of the losses. Strategically, however, the battle was a decisive British victory in that their control of the surface of the seas remained intact, the blockade unbroken. Indeed never again in the course of the war did the Germans come out to seek a fleet action. It could have been, and perhaps should have been, more total for the British. Material weaknesses (poor quality shells, lack of anti-flash precaution in the magazines, weak armour protection in the battlecruisers), tactical inflexibility, overcaution, downright lack of competence in certain instances, the misuse of intelligence and, above all, lack of knowledge of the enemy's position and strength (in days before radar) combined to rob them of outright victory. The German tactics in defence, on the other hand, were flexible and superbly conducted though the fact that they placed themselves in very compromising positions on two occasions lessens the claims of tactical genius on the part of their commanders.

Because the Battle of Jutland ended indecisively for the Germans, they were forced to consider other means of trying to wage the war at sea to a successful conclusion. While clashes of light forces continued in the Channel area for most of the remainder of the war, the overwhelming brunt of the German naval effort was switched to the submarine campaign against trade. Germany had, in fact, carried out two restricted

submarine campaigns prior to Jutland, but both had been ended when American protests assumed a severity that the Germans heeded. Nevertheless by 1917 with the German strategic position becoming increasingly difficult – deadlock on the Western Front, no prospects of victory in the east, the increasing effectiveness of the blockade and the growing numbness that came from the knowledge that things would get worse – the German Naval Staff estimated that on the basis of previous campaigns, German submarines could sink 600,000 tons of shipping a month. This, they estimated, would force the neutrals into breaking off their trade with Britain and, as a result, would force Britain out of the war. The calculation was that even if the USA entered the war as a result of unrestricted submarine warfare, Britain could be beaten before American intervention became effective. With the British out of the war, the French and Russians posed no real threat.

In the first half of the war German submarines had little difficulty in sinking merchantmen, if they were freed to do so by their orders. Submarines were able simply to patrol or wait on a sea lane knowing full well that sooner or later merchantmen would sail along it. While a submarine would move into the attack underwater, the most favoured method of sinking a ship was either by gunfire or by charges laid by a boarding party: commanders were loathe to use up their small supply of torpedoes against weak and inoffensive merchantmen. There was a problem in that a submarine had to surface to complete such tasks and there was the difficulty of identifying inoffensive merchantmen from those that were not since the British resorted to Q-ships (disguised merchantmen with strong gun armament whose role was to lure a submarine to point blank range by simulated panic and, when the enemy was close, to drop her disguise and destroy the submarine by overwhelming firepower or ramming).

The major British response to the submarine was relentless patrolling of the sea lanes, searching laboriously for elusive enemies that could usually slink away unnoticed since they had the advantage of first sighting. Such patrols operated under grave handicaps. Firstly, before 1916 there was no means of detecting or attacking a submerged submarine and even after that date, when hydrophones and depth charges were introduced, there remained many problems of operation that had to be overcome. Secondly, patrolling did not afford immediate protection to merchantmen since the latter remained undefended for the duration of their passage. In short, because of the British weakness, the only limitation on the number of merchantmen that could be sunk by German submarines was the endurance, weapons and orders of the submarines plus the number of Allied merchant ships sighted.

Such was the bankruptcy of British tactical ideas that in the first three months of the unrestricted submarine campaign, some two million tons of shipping were lost. The nadir of British fortunes came in April 1917 when 430 ships, totalling 843,549 tons were lost, the merchantman : submarine exchange ratio reaching 167 : 1. The U-boats were simply running amok and defeat was inevitable unless the British rapidly came up with some solution. With the Admiralty paralyzed by indecision it was left to the French and then the British prime minister to force an experiment with convoys on a reluctant British Admiralty.

Troop convoy had existed from the very start of the war effort, but although trade convoy had been instituted in previous wars in which the British had been involved, and its effectiveness recognized, its potential was at first ignored in World War I. (Trade convoy had been compulsory in many British wars, in fact, but the Admiralty's insistence on it was dropped in the nineteenth century in the belief that steam propulsion invalidated the concept: it was conveniently forgotten that the principles of war basically remain unchanged despite technical advances.) In fact the value of convoy was twofold. Firstly, a group of merchantmen under escort presented a single concentrated target. This meant that a submarine would have only one chance to sight the ships and only fleeting opportunities to attack some of them; the same number of ships sailing independently along the same course presented single sightings and easy targets. If the submarine failed to sight the convoy at all then the ships were safe. Secondly, in order to attack ships in convoy, the submarine had to come within range of escorts, thus exposing itself to counter-attack. Convoy therefore encouraged both a concentration of force on the part of the defence and an economy of effort since it meant that only the waters immediately around the convoy needed to be searched since it was in these waters that submarines were forced to operate in order to sink merchantmen. Overall, convoy forced submarines to attack strength, not weakness, under conditions increasingly less favourable to themselves.

Because of crippling losses towards the end of 1916 (40 per cent in December alone), the French in 1917 insisted that their coal trade with Britain had to be convoyed: without British coal French industry would have virtually collapsed. As a result of the introduction of convoys between southern England and France in 1917 losses fell abruptly. Under pressure from Lloyd George, the British premier, the Admiralty authorized oceanic convoy on April 26, 1917, the first convoy leaving Gibraltar for the UK on May 10; regular convoys were initiated in July. At the start the convoy

The RN crew and 'merchant' crew of 'Q' ship HMS *Hyderabad*. When 'Q' ships began to operate, U-boats would sink freighters with torpedoes but often surface afterwards. The 'merchant' crew would 'panic' and abandon the ship after contact with a U-boat and leave a skeleton crew (the RN crew) aboard to engage the submarine when she closed in.

system had two weaknesses. Contrary to common sense convoys were dispersed once in the Channel, for ships to sail independently for their home ports; outward-bound ships sailed independently. The basic strategic pattern, therefore, was to give protection right up to the point where it was most needed. It was not until August 1917 that outward convoys were initiated and not until November 1917 that convoy was extended right into selected ports. But gradually all of the most vulnerable routes – the Atlantic, Gibraltar-UK, the Mediterranean and UK coastal waters – were covered by two-way convoy.

Overall the results were startling. During the war the Germans sank nearly 13 million tons of shipping, $7\frac{3}{4}$ millions of which was British. But of the 16,070 ships that sailed in oceanic convoys only 96 were lost, and 161 were lost of the 67,888 sailings in coastal convoys. Losses among stragglers and independently sailed ships were much heavier but never of the order to give the Germans any chance of victory. Only five ships were lost when in the company of both sea and air escorts. In short convoy drastically cut losses. In November 1917 losses were the lowest they had been since the start of the campaign in February, despite the fact that in October German submarines reached the peak of their strength with seventy vessels at sea. By September 1918 losses had been cut to less than a hundred and in October 1918 only twenty-five Allied merchantmen were lost, though these figures do reflect the restrictions placed on submarine operations while the Germans sought an armistice. Not merely did convoy result in fewer ships being sunk – which meant that Allied shipbuilding could more than replace the losses –

but it enabled the Allies to start sinking U-boats on a large scale. That depth charges had claimed their first victim on March 26, 1916 and that the combination of depth charges and hydrophone made their first kill on July 6, 1916, were effective demonstrations that submarines could be effectively countered. The loss rate among U-boats between August 1917 and January 1918, when the issue was in the balance, was greater than German replacement capacity. At the same time the merchantmen:submarine exchange ratio fell to 10:1. Overall in the course of the war, 178 out of 373 German submarines were lost, most of them after the introduction of convoy.

Thus the strategic and tactical value of convoy was well illustrated by the events of World War I. The German submarine campaign failed not because of the considerable losses endured by the U-boats but as a result of the submarines being unable to maintain the high rate of sinkings that they had achieved between February and April 1917. Through a policy of convoy, ruthless rationing in the UK and the concentration of shipping on the critical US-UK trade route, the British were able to economize on their use of shipping. The Germans were also hampered by Allied counter-measures in the Channel where the mine barriers were considerably strengthened and patrols increased in order to prevent the Germans passing through the Straits of Dover. Instead they were forced to move to and from Germany to the battle zones via the north of Scotland, a time consuming route with few targets to make the passage profitable. By such methods the Allies were able to deny the Germans the strategic victory they sought – and the failure to win on the sea

routes made the German defeat even more certain as American forces began to pour into Europe in the spring of 1918. Nevertheless, despite this failure, the U-boats did serve to tie down the light forces of the Allies on escort duties and, as such, they were unable to take part in any proposal to make more aggressive use of Allied sea power.

In theory, given the possession of superior sea power and the advantage of external lines of communication, the Allies should have been able to use the great flexibility of sea power to impose their will on the enemy by a series of independent seaborne assaults. In practice, the short coastline of Germany and Austro-Hungary, combined with the power of mines and torpedoes, made these countries almost totally invulnerable to seaborne assault. The first few months of the war were characterized by a restless search for a naval offensive on the part of the British Admiralty, partly in the hope that this would force the Germans to come out to give battle, partly in order to force the enemy to conform to British strategic intentions. Various schemes were proposed, most of them nonsensical. There were schemes to seize a German island in the North Sea – or a Dutch island or Danish or Norwegian town, it did not seem to matter too much; there was a proposal to launch a one-way raid up the Elbe to attack Hamburg and the Brunsbuttel and Kiel Canals; there were schemes for landing on the Schleswig-Holstein coast and in the Baltic, though how these operations were to be carried out in the face of German and Danish mines without much in the field of destroyer protection, was not seriously considered at the outset. Subsequently, all were found to have problems so severe that they had

to be dropped: it is hard to resist the conclusion that they should not have been considered in the first place. Leaving aside the contemptibly incompetent landings at Tanga in November 1914, the British carried out only one major attempt to get around the German land flanks by the use of sea power. That was with the brilliantly imaginative and totally unrealistic operation at the Dardanelles.

From the very inception of the campaign, there were three strategic weaknesses in the arguments in favour. Firstly, while admitting that the longest way around is often the shortest way there, the notion of dealing a fatal blow at Germany via Turkey – the knocking away of the props – implied a relationship between Germany and Turkey that did not exist. The central problem in defeating Germany had to be the German Army, not Turkey. Striking at a place where the Germans could not strike back had, as its penalty, striking at a place where the Germans could not be touched. Moreover, the notion that the Balkan states could provide the key to victory by opening up a further front is dubious in that, rather than providing support for the Allies, these countries could easily have become liabilities and obligations to be met. Secondly, the operation was carried out at a time when the British (and French) lacked the strength to maintain an effort on even one front, still less a second at the far end of the Mediterranean. The Dardanelles operation was an attempt to gain a victory on the cheap and in attempting this the Allies expended more effort overall than was ever realistically needed for a thorough and properly prepared operation in the first place. Moreover, even if the operation had been successful, and access gained

to south Russian ports, it is hard to see where the ships and supplies that were supposed to keep Russia magically in the war could have come from, granted the fact that most shipping and arms suppliers were committed already to the British and French causes. Thirdly, and lastly, the notion that developed in the winter of 1914-15 that the Navy alone could force the Dardanelles was in flat contradiction to staff appreciations before 1914; all of which stressed that any operation at the Dardanelles was bound to be hazardous and demand a joint Army-Navy effort. In the winter of 1914 a state of euphoria, reckless personal ambition and irresponsibility on the part of Churchill, a large measure of downright ignorance of, and racial contempt for, the Turks, led to the evolution of a plan for a solely naval offensive. Yet any such offensive fell foul to two immediate considerations. Firstly, even if the fleet managed to force its way up the Dardanelles there was no guarantee that this could be turned to a decisive strategic success unless its flanks were cleared: the flanks could only be cleared, and held, by the Army. Secondly, the essence of the problem of forcing the Dardanelles was that mines blocked the passage and were covered by guns. Because of the fast flow of water the primitive minesweepers could not clear the mines because of the unacceptable volume of firepower they had to face. This gunfire could not be suppressed by the remainder of the fleet because the minefields prevented close range action on the part of the ships. The only way to break the vicious circle was to take the guns covering the minefields from the landside – by using the Army to seize the enemy positions. Churchill, intoxicated by the early successes of the Navy against the dilapidated outer defences, pushed forward with the plan for a solely naval attack. The steady crumbling of the defences came to a halt on March 11, 1915 with the Navy unable to make any more progress. There followed an ominous lull in British deliberations while the questions of whether or not to mount an invasion, and in what strength, were discussed, and arrangements put in hand. On March 18 a final effort was made by the Navy with eighteen battleships including the brand new *Queen Elizabeth*, to break through the still intact defences. It was very nearly successful, in that the Turks came close to exhausting their ammunition in fighting off the ships, but in the course of the action three capital ships were lost and three more badly crippled. The naval commander was unwilling to risk more of his ships in a final effort that could have proved

decisive – throughout the operation greater emphasis seems to have been placed on ship preservation than in recognition of the fact that losses could be endured if the strategic objective was gained. In mitigation it must be noted that the cause of the losses was unknown at the time and the weakness of the Turkish situation on land was obviously not realized. With the Army unready to begin operations the attacks had to be called off for the moment and it was not until April 25, 1915 that landings on the Gallipoli peninsula took place. Many things went wrong: some landings took place on the wrong beaches, fire support from ships was insufficient because of the inadequacies of fire control, and toal chaos reigned on V beach where the assaulting infantry were cut down in swathes by intact machine guns. But in spite of this the critically important village of Krithia could have been taken on the 25th, and the commanding height of Achi Baba might well have been taken on several occasions. Had the latter fallen, the outcome may well have been very different but in fact it was held throughout by the Turks. Ultimately, despite heroic efforts on the part of the land forces the British had to admit failure and the peninsula was progressively evacuated with superbly executed withdrawals that were carried out without a single casualty, despite the presence of the enemy.

The Dardanelles operation illustrates the limitations

of sea power and the extent to which it is dependent on proper co-ordination with other services. In the actual details of the operation, the need was shown for specialized headquarters ships for amphibious operations: part of the difficulties encountered on April 25 stemmed from having Army headquarters on board a ship that had its own tasks to complete. The landing underlined the need for proper fire control arrangements and landing craft and, equally, the importance of proper loading and shipping arrangements to ensure that the most important supplies were loaded last and delivered first. In addition, the need for adequate medical facilities was appallingly obvious for those at the Dardanelles would not have done justice to the Crimea.

Nevertheless the Dardanelles on several occasions did come very close to being a decisive British success.

Had more care been taken in the initial stages it might well have been a measure that knocked Turkey out of the war, and might have brought about the situation that some of its proponents assert would have occurred. But this is conjecture. What is certain, is that the Dardanelles notched up an impressive series of 'firsts': for the first time a submarine sank a battleship with torpedoes; the first aerial spotting for guns occurred; and for the first time aircraft sank ships on the open sea with plenty of searoom. Though there were other advances in other theatres – for instance in the Baltic both the Russians and the Germans used aerial mines – the Dardanelles marked the debut of the weapon that was to figure largely in the inter-war tactical and strategic arguments, and that was to dominate war at sea between 1939 and 1945.

Exit the Battleship enter the Carrier

HMS *Hermes* in 1937 passes through the Suez Canal. She was the first ship designed from the keel up as a carrier for the Royal Navy.

It has already been recounted how the long period of Victorian peace, then the revolution in material at the turn of the century, was not conducive to the study of war at sea. Strategy was neglected and tactical thought has been described scathingly as 'a few catchwords and a lot of tradition.' In the period between the two wars strategic and tactical thought was similarly stifled and also distorted – though for very different reasons and never to the extent that it had been prior to 1914.

In part this resulted from three major considerations. Firstly, though there were periodic scares, none of the navies in the immediate post-war era could point to 'the next enemy' against whom preparations had to be made. It was not until the thirties that events began to take shape that clarified the nature of the future conflict and made possible the identification of the likely enemies. Secondly, the inter-war period was dominated by economies in the naval services and international agreements that resulted in the cutting back of naval strengths generally, both of which had the effect of dampening initiative, drive and new ideas. Thirdly, there was a natural tendency to fight the battles of World War I over again – this was particularly true of the British and the Battle of Jutland. In a very real sense the emphasis of British naval thought and training in the inter-war period was devoted to making sure that in future similar opportunities would not be missed. The results were very impressive: in numerous actions during World War II British gunnery and night fighting proved extremely formidable; the elan and initiative of the light forces, so conspicuously lacking at Jutland, exhibited themselves at every opportunity; and in battle there was frequent demonstration of flexibility of

command, partly, it must be added, as a result of the development of radar which, with radio, enabled the commander to know more about the battle area in spite of high speed manoeuvring than had been possible in the past. Naval thought, on the other hand, was distorted by two factors. Firstly, little attention was paid to economic warfare, particularly in the field of trade defence against submarine attack. In the whole of the inter-war period the Royal Navy conducted only one exercise in trade defence. Such complacency stemmed partly from the belief that convoy was the effective answer to submarines and partly in the confidence placed in ASDIC (later called Sonar) as the means of detecting a submerged submarine. (This had been invented towards the end of World War I.) The British particularly, believed that it was the antidote to the submarine. Secondly, furious arguments raged over the questions of the role and importance of naval aviation, questions inevitably tied up with arguments about the role of air power in general.

In the inter-war period naval thought essentially divided into four major streams on the vexed problem of naval aviation, with many shades of opinion in between. On one extreme were those who believed that air power made the existing battle fleets and most of the surface ships obsolete; on the other those whose belief in gunnery led to their discounting the aircraft as a serious factor in war at sea. Between the two extremes was an area of doubt. Although there could be no doubt that an aircraft could physically sink a battleship – the American general Billy Mitchell had shown that in trials with the *Ostfriesland* in 1921 – there was a school of thought which was of the opinion that,

given better protection (particularly in deck and water-line armour), improved damage control arrangements, more and better high angle guns and, if possible, organic air defence, the role of the battleship as the principle weapon at sea could remain unchallenged. Within this school it was felt that air power was very important indeed and that the destructive capability of aircraft was second only to the guns of the fleet – but it was clearly secondary, for to them air power existed to provide air defence for the battle line, to spot for the guns of the fleet. Aircraft, too, could push out the range of reconnaissance several hundreds of miles, effectively reducing the importance of the cruiser in this role. The final major stream of thought reasoned that not only would the range of reconnaissance be pushed out several hundreds of miles, but that there was the distinct possibility, even probability, that any engagement between the battle lines would be preceded by an air battle, the outcome of which might in itself be conclusive. For the most part this school shrank from the

ultimate logic of its line of argument, that indeed the aircraft had made the battle line obsolete, though many officers suspected (or hoped) that this either was or shortly would be the case. Such reasoning inevitably pointed towards a concept of naval warfare in which the battle fleet would be led by a carrier force committed to fighting for air supremacy: it was towards this conclusion that the Japanese and Americans were gingerly feeling their way during the inter-war period.

While the Japanese and the Americans forged ahead in the theory and practice of naval aviation, the British by comparison stagnated – a fact possibly not unrelated to the fact that the Royal Navy lost its own fleet air arm to the Royal Air Force while the American and Japanese Navies retained total control of their own naval aviation. The war-time British lead in ships operating aircraft, and in numbers and types of aircraft, was quickly dissipated. In 1918 they had 1000 aircraft and lighter-than-air machines; a year of peace and demobilization reduced this total to fifty. Although after

1918 the British were the first to build a ship with a continuous free flight deck (the *Argus*), and to have a carrier with an offset island in order to clear smoke from the flight deck (the *Eagle*), it was the Japanese who were the first to complete a purpose-built carrier (the *Hosho*) in 1922, and it was the Pacific powers that attempted to produce specialist aircraft. Whereas the British tended to rely on multi-purpose aircraft that could never perform any task really well, the Japanese and Americans set out to create specialist torpedo, fighter and reconnaissance and, later, dive bomber formations. The result was that over time, Japanese and American aircraft opened up a considerable qualitative gap between themselves and British naval aircraft, this becoming particularly marked during the thirties with the introduction of the monoplane into the American and Japanese Navies. In only two areas did the British continue to possess a lead: they had many more carriers than the other two countries (though this advantage was offset by the greater carrying capacity of the US and Japan), and their carriers had the supreme advantage of heavily armoured flight deck, hangars and magazines.

When rearmament began apace in the second half of the thirties, it was perhaps inevitable that first priority was given to carriers, the battle line (no nation was willing to risk abandoning battleships), cruisers and destroyers. Even the British largely went along with such priorities though it must be noted that the 1939 War Emergency, 1940 and 1941 Programmes placed great emphasis on destroyer escorts, frigates and corvettes. These ships were specifically built for the protection of trade since it was on this front that Britain faced her greatest test. The threat of course came from Germany. In 1937 Germany set out a construction programme for her rejuvenated navy of six battleships, three battlecruisers, four heavy cruisers, seventeen light cruisers, four carriers, numerous destroyers and two hundred and twenty-one submarines. The date when these ships were to be ready was 1948. This fleet was not intended to fight in the classic manner for supremacy at sea: it was aimed primarily at the destruction of British trade – either by the physical sinking of ships or by the prevention of ships even sailing because of the unrestricted presence of German warships on the high seas. Given the fact that forty-eight British warships had to be committed to the destruction of the *Bismarck* in May 1941, and that two of the battleships proposed in 1937 were half as big again as the *Bismarck*, the Germans may well have achieved their objective had

war come later rather than in 1939 when their construction programmes had barely started.

The war certainly came too early for Karl Doenitz the commander of the German submarine arm. He knew exactly what he wanted since he alone clearly appreciated the vulnerability of Britain's sea communications. He realized that submarines operating independently dissipated much of their value. He realized, too, that the principle of concentration of force worked for both the defender and the attacker. Before the war Doenitz trained his submarines to operate in groups, initially in a long extended concave patrol line into which an enemy convoy would enter. The submarine making the first sighting would report the enemy and direct the other members of the group on to the convoy in order to attack it from the flanks and rear. The favoured position of the shadowing submarine was naturally behind the convoy. In carrying out attacks on convoys the submarines came to prefer approaches and attacks on the surface at night, even to the extent in some cases of entering the lines of merchantmen and attacking the convoy from the inside. In attempting this the submarine commanders were confident that once inside the convoy they would be immune from attack since the escorts would be too concerned with perimeter defence. In attempting to get inside the convoy the submarines had the advantage of first sighting since their low silhouettes against a dark sea made them hard to detect while the escorts and merchantmen could be seen far more easily. In this role the submarines were employed as torpedo boats that could dive to avoid an escort rather than as a submerged craft *per se*. Moreover, attacking on the surface made submarines invulnerable to detection by ASDIC. Doenitz wanted to stake all on a submarine campaign against British trade and he wanted priority given to the 300 submarines he deemed necessary to force Britain to her knees. He reckoned that of this total one-third would be on station at any given time, the remainder equally divided between vessels moving to and from operations and those undergoing refits, training and 'or leave'. In addition, he wanted small 500-ton submarines armed with about fourteen torpedoes. The smallness of these vessels made them very manoeuvrable and they were able to submerge in twenty seconds. Unfortunately for Doenitz the German Navy did not agree with his order of priorities and in any case were inclined to build larger submarines with strong gun armament and long endurance. Doenitz went to war with only fifty-six

The German battleship *Bismarck* at the beginning of her first and last cruise. German naval doctrine was to destroy British shipping with U-boats and powerful surface vessels like the *Bismarck*. If they sank enough they would starve Britain into surrender.

submarines, some of which were totally unsuited to long-range operations.

Doenitz's opponents, on the other hand, were fatally weak. The British had less than thirty escort ships in the Western Approaches when war broke out, and less than one hundred overall. They could not easily be reinforced by fleet destroyers since these ships were needed for other tasks and were in any case not easily adaptable to escort duties. Given their fleet role, destroyers tended to be high speed craft with heavy gun, anti-aircraft and torpedo armament: for defence of convoys endurance, small turning circles and good anti-

submarine weapons were needed. Moreover the performance of ASDIC tended to fall away at high speed. In addition to these handicaps the British operated under two severe difficulties. Firstly, the British government during the 1930s relinquished its treaty ports in Eire, with the result that escorts had to work out of home ports; secondly, the Royal Navy had neglected replenishment at sea (RAS) and a fleet train during the inter-war period (in marked contrast to the Americans and Japanese). This meant that British escorts could give support for convoys only within 600 miles of the UK coast; beyond this the merchantmen

were more or less on their own until they approached
the New World. Such were the major weaknesses of the
two sides in September 1939.

World War II: General Comment

World War II was essentially two quite separate wars:
one fought basically in Europe and the Atlantic, the
other in the West and South Pacific (and certain parts
of the Asian mainland). Only very occasionally did the
two overlap and then in no meaningful strategic sense.
The wars were largely fought in isolation of each other,
the unifying factor being the involvement of the
British and Americans (and to a lesser extent the
French and Soviets) in both conflicts. In large measure,
events shaped the strategies of Germany, Japan and
Britain. Germany, given the British unwillingness to
come to terms in 1940 and lacking a surface navy of real
strength, was forced into unrestricted submarine warfare against British trade. For the most part the British
strategy was defensive in that the Navy had to struggle
to secure the homeland against direct invasion and to
keep open the trade routes with the rest of the world.
The maintenance of her sea communications was at the
very heart of Britain's survival and capacity for any kind
of offensive action: if they had been severed she would
have had to surrender. Except in the secondary
Mediterranean theatre, British naval policy was defensive and, given the absence of a balanced German fleet
and a determined Italian naval effort, the European war
at sea was fought along the trade routes between British
(and Allied) escorts and German submarines (and aircraft). There were surface actions and the Germans
used their surface ships to try to pin down British
forces, particularly the escorts, in order to facilitate the
tasks of the submarines, but for the most part this was a
secondary effort. Japan, in 1941, was similarly committed by the march of events. Because of her over-
commitment and the elusiveness of decisive strategic
success in China, the thrashing administered her by the
Soviet Union in Mongolia in 1939, her desperate
reliance on the resources of South-East Asia, and
American opposition to her that hardened implacably
during the course of 1941, she was forced to attempt
the neutralization of American naval power and the
provision of a distant defensive perimeter, held by the
carriers and battle fleet, behind which she could exploit
the natural resources of her intended conquests. The
Japanese Commander-in-Chief, Admiral Yamamoto,

was not sanguine about the prospects of such a plan,
but he had no option. Japan could hardly attempt the
conquest of South-East Asia with the American battle
fleet intact on her left flank and the American possession of the Philippines astride the sea routes between
South-East Asia and Japan. Yamamoto doubted
whether Japan could hold the US Navy once the
Americans fully mobilized their industrial resources, so
infinitely superior to those of Japan and had cause to
ponder the immense problems of forming a defensive
perimeter consisting mostly of sea and sky without the
necessary merchant and naval ships needed to give that
perimeter teeth. In addition, the policy of securing a
defensive line and then standing on the defence for the
counter-attack against an enemy superior in strength
and resources had little to recommend it. But the
Japanese had no choice: their foreign policy in the
thirties drove them into the cul-de-sac of the early
forties.

The Americans, on the other hand, did have
strategic choice, largely conferred by their geographical
isolation and invulnerability. Before the war they had
drawn up a series of war plans to cover every possible
contingency (including war with Britain) and had
decided that, in the event of war in both the Pacific and
Europe, priority should be placed on the latter. The
decision was made on the basis that any Japanese
victories could be redeemed in time whereas a German
victory in Europe could prove final and irreversible.
When war came to the USA in 1941 these priorities
were confirmed and maintained, though the revelation
of Japanese weakness in 1942-3 enabled the Americans
to undertake a more vigorous and aggressive policy on
both fronts than they had considered possible before the
war. Such a situation arose not simply because of
Japan's inherent weaknesses but because of the seemingly inexhaustible capacity of American industry: in
1942 and 1943 it was completing a destroyer every three
days; in the last quarter of 1943, merchant ship construction was running at an annual rate of 16.4 million
tons. At the end of the war American shipyards were
building aircraft carriers that, had they been completed,
would have almost doubled the Navy's carrier strength
of twenty-three fleet carriers.

Such strength was witness to the eclipse of British
sea power, finally relegated to the second rank for the
first time in 250 years. It also marked the end of the
domination of the battleship. Admittedly for the operations against the Marianas in 1944, the Americans were

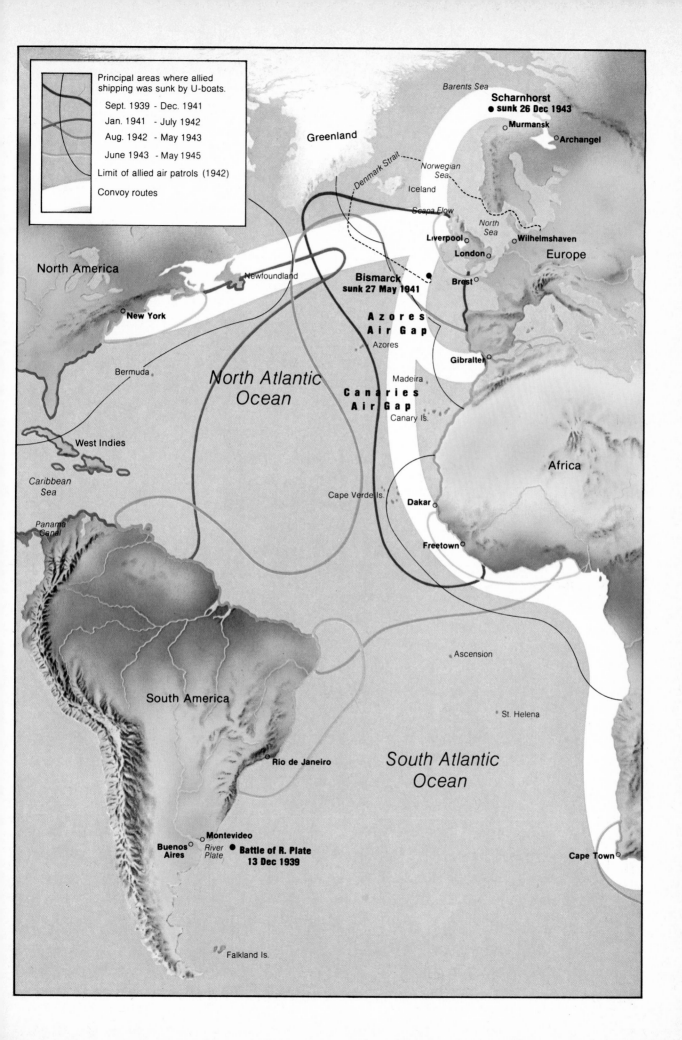

Principal areas where allied shipping was sunk by U-boats.

Sept. 1939 - Dec. 1941

Jan. 1941 - July 1942

Aug. 1942 - May 1943

June 1943 - May 1945

Limit of allied air patrols (1942)

Convoy routes

Barents Sea

Scharnhorst
● sunk 26 Dec 1943

Murmansk

Archangel

Greenland

Denmark Strait

Norwegian Sea

Iceland

Scapa Flow

North Sea

Liverpool

London

Europe

Wilhelmshaven

Bismarck sunk 27 May 1941

Brest

North America

Newfoundland

A z o r e s A i r G a p

Azores

Gibraltar

New York

North Atlantic Ocean

Bermuda

Madeira

C a n a r i e s A i r G a p

Canary Is.

Africa

West Indies

Caribbean Sea

Cape Verde Is.

Dakar

Panama Canal

Freetown

Ascension

South America

St. Helena

Rio de Janeiro

South Atlantic Ocean

Montevideo

Buenos Aires

River Plate

● **Battle of R. Plate 13 Dec 1939**

Cape Town

Falkland Is.

The *Admiral Graf Spee*, the so-called 'pocket battleship' because her weight was only 12,100 tons, but she had six 11-in (280 mm) guns and could reach 27.7 knots. A potent commerce raider, she was scuttled after the Battle of the River Plate in 1939.

able to deploy fourteen battleships (more than the Royal Navy had in commission at the time) and they were able to play a vital role, but the real teeth of the navies from this point was in the carriers and their aircraft. (In the Marianas operation the Americans employed fifteen fleet carriers and ten light carriers.) Gradually the battleship was relegated to the second rank – important primarily in pre-invasion bombardment and for close fire support for land forces once ashore, and with a vital role in defence of convoys (the unsung British R class saved many convoys from annihilation at the hands of German surface raiders simply by being there). They could also provide vital cover for the carriers against both surface and air attack: indeed carriers with their lack of guns and vulnerability often sought the comfort and reassurance of massed anti-aircraft batteries of battleships. But these were all secondary tasks: the role of finding and destroying the enemy fleet had passed to the carriers.

The European War

From the very start of the war the British and French Navies were engaged in imposing blockade on Germany and in convoying military formations to areas of operations both in Europe and throughout the world. The latter particularly affected the French and their possessions in North Africa, as did the need to keep watch on unpredictable but unfriendly Italy. The imposition of blockade was naturally the main task of the British, who used exactly the same methods as they had in World War I – patrolling in the Channel, the fleet based at Scapa Flow and the northern patrol of armed merchant cruisers. In World War II, however, blockade never had anything like the devastating effect that

it had had in World War I. This was partly due to German stockpiling before the war, partly because of German development of effective substitutes for many now missing goods, partly the outcome of the Nazi-Soviet honeymoon of 1939-41 which meant that trade with the USSR more than offset any losses caused by blockade. And it also stemmed in part from the sheer extent of German conquests and her rapacious stripping of these conquered territories. It was not really until the end of the war that she began to feel the full rigour of economic shortages; by the time that economic collapse did occur, she had been decisively defeated on land and, in any case, the contribution of air power to her economic collapse was more spectacular, immediate and profound than that of naval blockade.

At the start of the war Hitler did not launch complete all-out submarine warfare. Restrictions were placed on the sinking of merchant ships though these were progressively relaxed as it became obvious that the Allies and later Britain alone would not come to terms. In the early months of the war the Germans used mine warfare off the east coast and surface ships, both naval and auxiliary, in the prosecution of war against commerce. After 1941 the effectiveness of surface raiders greatly diminished as British counter-measures, particularly in the fields of intelligence and the checking of identity of individual ships encountered by naval units on the high seas, gradually improved. In their heyday the surface ships had some considerable success in stopping or disrupting the flow of convoys rather than inflicting losses through the auxiliaries *Atlantis* and *Pinguin*, and the warships *Scharnhorst* and *Gneisenau* in the January-March 1941 operations enjoyed considerable success (a total of sixty-two ships of about 400,000 tons sunk). But submarines, despite their role against

Below: A coastal U-boat. By 1940 Germany had bases for submarine war, but not enough vessels to wage it. Had Doenitz been allowed to build up the U-boat fleet before 1939 the outcome of World War II might have been very different. Bottom: On the lookout in the Atlantic. The advent of radar removed the cover of darkness and poor weather that had been used by the U-boats for stalking.

the British fleet, were the main means of striking at British trade, and as more submarines entered service, Allied losses mounted. Nearly 4 million tons were lost in 1940, half to submarines: roughly the same figures were reported for 1941. In the first thirty months of the war German submarines had things much their own way. Strategically, the Germans concentrated on the UK-US and coastal UK trade routes, and their possession after mid-1940 of bases in Norway and western France enabled their submarines to reach out into the Atlantic far beyond the range of most British escorts. In effect, the Germans were blockading Britain as they had in World War I but from a position of much greater strength than had been possible between 1914 and 1918. Forty-nine per cent of all Allied losses between 1939 and mid-1942 were in the North Atlantic; between 1939 and mid-1941 32 per cent of all Allied losses were in and around UK coastal waters. Tactically, the only limitation on German submarines was the scarcity of the submarines themselves, the lack of co-operation from the Luftwaffe, and the small numbers of torpedoes they could carry. In carrying out this scale of destruction the U-boats enjoyed considerable immunity: only twenty-three submarines were lost in 1940 and only thirty-five in the whole of 1941. And in the last quarter of 1941, replacement exceeded the whole of the losses suffered during the war to date. In the first two years of the war the paucity of escorts, their limited range and, most importantly, the fact that they were seldom ever able to train together but were put in teams on the basis of what was available rather than what was needed, meant that the escorts laboured under immense difficulties. By the end of 1941 the situation at sea was becoming increasingly grave for the British. Merchantmen were being lost twice as quickly as they could be replaced; German U-boat strength was nearing 250 with about 97 at sea at any one time. Clearly things were moving towards a climax.

Two developments took place in the course of 1941 that showed that U-boats need not necessarily have things all their own way. Firstly, between July and

U-boat hunters in the Atlantic: Top left: HMS *Hydrangea* a Flower Class corvette. Top right: The destroyer HMS *Scimitar* and Bottom: HMS *Walker* a veteran of World War I. During escort duties with convoy HX112 in March 1941, she depth charged U-99 and captured her commander the 'ace' Otto Kretschmer.

December, losses on the North Atlantic route fell to about 100,000 tons a month – an indication of the growing presence of American strength in the western and central Atlantic where Germany feared to move because of the obvious danger of war with the US. But the decline of losses was also an indication that convoys were becoming more effective. Secondly, and related to the latter point, in December 1941 a convoy of thirty-two ships was fought through from Gibraltar to the UK with the loss of only two ships. Two escorts were also lost but five German submarines and two aircraft were destroyed. This convoy (HG 76) was exceptionally well defended, however, leaving Gibraltar with 10 escorts and a small escort carrier. It was commanded by the most famous of the British escort commanders, Captain F. J. Walker, and clearly showed what an aggressive, balanced and well-trained force trained together could achieve, particularly when supported by a carrier.

Despite HG 76 the convoy system came under great strain in 1942 and the first quarter of 1943, because of

the extension of the war through the Atlantic and Pacific areas. This stretched Anglo-American resources far beyond their capacity and it took some time for the Americans to organize themselves and begin to draw on their potential strength. When the tide turned spectacularly in the spring of 1943 it was the result of a combination of factors, many of which had been clearly seen with the success of HG 76.

The nature of the victory of the convoy system was two-fold. Firstly, the Allies halted the massive scale of sinkings that took place in early 1943, which would have forced Britain out of the war had it persisted. Allied measures proved successful in preventing a rate of loss that could not be covered by fresh American construction. Secondly, German submarines in 1943 took losses that were totally unacceptable – 237 for the year, including 41 at the climax of the battle in May.

Of all the factors that contributed to the Allied victory on the sea routes probably the most important was the provision of more and better trained escorts.

A depth charge with quick-sinking attachment. Used in two world wars, it was very effective once a definite contact had been made with a submerged U-boat. Dropped or projected in a pattern and set for different depths, they would explode causing pressures that would crush the hull of a U-boat.

Early convoys proved fatally weak in escorts with all too predictable results. By 1943 more escorts were available with the result that the perimeter defence of convoys was far better. It was also realized that, tactically, an area of convoy (and hence the number of merchant ships in it) could be greatly increased relative to the perimeter by an increase in radius (the mathematical formula for area of circle as opposed to the circumference) and that there was an optimum size for a convoy and its escorts. The result of such deductions enabled strong defences to be prepared for convoys and even led to the formation of 'trouble-shooters' that could patrol routes to and from the U-boat bases or submarine-infested waters, giving aid to any convoy in the vicinity.

Technologically, too, the balance shifted away from the submarines in the course of the war. The development of radar and its use by escorts gave the defender the critical advantage of identifying the submarine before, and not after, its attack: the submarine thereby lost its immunity and the advantage of first sighting. Moreover, new weapons began to appear during the course of the war: mortars capable of firing twenty-four contact bombs, forward-throwing fast-sinking depth charges, depth charges with a 500-ft capability – all began to take an increasing toll. Part of the problem in destroying a submarine in the early years of the war had been that an escort in contact with it by ASDIC lost that contact as it moved into the attack, and also gave notice of intent by the sound of its engines; an alert submarine could therefore always try to turn away from the attack at the last moment. The new weapons allowed ASDIC to maintain contact as the contact was made. Walker developed one particular ploy to overcome the U-boats' evasive manoeuvres even before the new weapons came into service on a large scale: he used an escort to hold contact and to bring two or three other escorts at very slow speeds either across or over the U-boat, depth charging along both the U-boat line itself and either side of it. In this way any late evasive action brought the submarine into the line of depth charges to the side of its original course. No German submarine ever survived such an attack.

Walker was also notable for his aggressive defence, even when he had small forces at his disposal. The defence of HG 76 unveiled the hitherto unheard of tactic of weakening the defence screen in an effort to keep down or destroy the submarine with the first contact; he also encouraged aggressive lunges at U-boats moving into the attack, even if this meant further weakening the defences. As more escorts became available more aggressive action around the perimeter was possible; Walker was exceptional in that he employed such tactics when such strength was not available. Such was the effectiveness of the escorts in this role that the Germans were forced to develop accoustic torpedoes designed to home on to the sound of ship propellers. They intended to use their limited supply of such torpedoes against the escorts with a view to clearing a route through to the merchantmen. Some initial success was achieved, mainly because of the element of surprise, but several tactical ploys were evolved to overcome their effectiveness. Noise-making equipment was developed that could be towed astern of the escorts to draw off the torpedoes (the weakness of this was that it interfered with ASDIC); (Walker's preference) high or low speed steaming when the effectiveness of the torpedoes fell away; or the dropping of depth charges to detonate the torpedoes themselves.

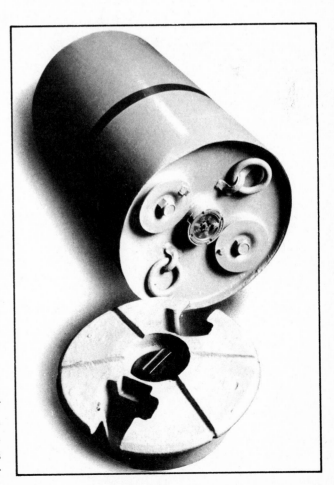

The death of a U-boat. Caught on the surface by an RAF aircraft it has been depth charged and machine-gunned. German submarines had been built with the assumption that they would operate under friendly or neutral skies and unlike their British counterparts were slower at crash dives. Depth charges with a shallow setting could rupture the pressure hull on or just below the surface.

A further factor in the decisive Allied success in the Battle of the Atlantic was the advent of air power on a major scale in the course of 1943. In the early years the British effort was severely handicapped by the lack of either shore- or ship-based aircraft on any scale. Aircraft for convoy work were vital in three respects: firstly, to try to prevent reconnaissance and bombing by the Luftwaffe, (which became increasingly less effective as the strength of the Luftwaffe was sapped in the course of the war); secondly, for aggressive patrolling of the perimeter; and thirdly, for general attacks on surfaced submarines. In the early part of the war aircraft were simply not available. One expediency was to arm merchant ships with a single catapulted fighter but this could not be recovered and there were considerable problems involved in deciding to produce a weapon that could never be used again. It was not until 1943 that the solutions began to appear in strength. A massive in-

crease in long-range aircraft operating from the UK, Iceland and the New World (and later the Azores) enabled the Allies to cover the whole of the Atlantic, thus denying German submarines a safe area in which to run on the surface in order to recharge their batteries, and enabling the convoys to have some protection for parts of their passage. After 1943 such aircraft were equipped with either 1.5m or 10cm radar sets and were able to locate a surface U-boat in the foulest weather or at night; and shallow-depth charges gave them a means of destruction totally lacking up until that time. By 1943 not only were shore-based aircraft increasing in numbers and effectiveness, but continuous air cover was being provided by growing numbers of rugged little escort carriers, mostly American built. Very small with about fifteen to twenty aircraft, these ships could sweep the areas around the convoys – particularly to the rear where submarines tended to concentrate and where the escorts were naturally weak. Although their anti-submarine armament was weak, their ability to search and direct escorts proved a major factor in increasing the effectiveness of convoy protection. Such was the decisive impact of Allied air power that, in 1943, aircraft accounted for 116 German submarines.

German tactics as a result of this changing balance of technology were hesitant. In the crisis of 1943, as German submarines came under increasingly frequent and heavy air attack, they were armed with more and heavier anti-aircraft guns and were ordered to move together to provide mutual protection. This proved ineffective: aircraft took heavy losses but still managed to sink them. The only answers available were the snorkel, which allowed a submarine to recharge its batteries and change its air while still submerged, or the development of new submarines. The snorkel was used extensively after 1943 but only at the price of low submerged speeds and decreased fighting effectiveness; the new submarines which emerged in 1945 came too late to reverse the tide.

The war in the Mediterranean was similarly a war largely fought along the sea lanes – the British sea lanes to Malta and the Italian-German convoy routes from Europe to North Africa. Few campaigns illustrate more graphically the critical importance of sea power and the inter-dependence between the land, sea and air theatres than this campaign. Put at its simplest, the armies in North Africa were utterly dependent on sea power for their supplies. Given the superior geographical position of Italy, and the shortness of the Axis sea routes to North Africa, the British had to sever this supply route for the army to have any chance of clearing the North African coast. This could only be achieved if naval forces operated out of Malta – and Malta could be supplied only with difficulty as long as the North African coast remained in hostile hands. Air cover for a convoy would be minimal as long as the British did not hold the Western Desert. In this case the chances of resupplying Valetta were very poor. Ultimately the war in the Mediterranean lasted some three years, in the course of which both Italian and British merchant seamen displayed persistence and bravery of the highest order, matched only by the sacrifice and gallantry of escorts on both sides.

In the first six months of the war, the British had things much their own way. The heavy ships of the Italian Navy were timidly handled and in the early exchanges the British achieved a striking moral ascendancy over the Italians that the latter never fully shook off, even in later months. In large part Italian difficulties stemmed from their lack of a naval aviation arm; relations between the Italian Navy and Air Force were, to put it mildly, erratic. The British, especially when they had carriers, were far better served, though on many occasions, particularly in 1941, the Royal Navy had to operate with no air cover at all – as in Greece and Crete where twenty-two warships and five transports were sunk or severely damaged, and a further fourteen ships were less extensively damaged.

In the opening exchanges, the British dominated the central Mediterranean by aggressive sweeps in order to lure out the superior Italian fleet to a battle the British were convinced they would win decisively. No engagement ever took place, however, the Italian battle fleet declining action wherever possible. They were badly shaken by the aggressiveness of the British and by such actions as the Toranto attack of November when the British used carrier aircraft against the Italian battle line in harbour: the Italians lost three battleships in this attack. Respect for British naval aviation was further enhanced in March 1941 off Cape Matapan when Royal Navy and Royal Air Force aircraft delivered up part of the enemy battle fleet in flight to the guns of the pursuing British battle line – just as the *Bismark* was to be cornered and destroyed by avenging Home Fleet units in May 1941 after having been crippled by torpedo-plane attack.

At Matapan the Italians lost three fine cruisers and two heavy destroyers and were perhaps lucky not to lose more. Fighting blindly and without air cover, they were extremely prudent in their subsequent actions – on no occasion more so than at the second battle of Sirte in March 1942. In order to fight in a convoy of four merchant ships to Malta from Alexandria, the British provided a cruiser and six destroyers as close escort and a covering force that at one time numbered four cruisers and ten destroyers. The Italians put in ineffective air and torpedo-boat attacks but placed their faith in a force of one battleship, two cruisers one light cruiser and four destroyers. The British were organized as close escort, a smokescreen laying force and five divisions intending to stand out from the convoy if it was threatened. When the Italian cruisers were sighted the convoy turned away under cover of smoke that was blown by a rising 25-knot wind. The British divisions repelled the first attack but when the battleship came up, the Italians attempted to

Left: Part of the main armament of the German battlecruiser *Scharnhorst.* **She was ordered to see to attack the British Convoy JW55B, but naval intelligence and shrewd tactics enabled the British to deploy ships whose combined firepower sank the battle cruiser on December 26, 1943. Right: Mundane sea-power, a motorcycle comes ashore from a British LCM.**

work their way around the smokescreen (which they naturally feared entering) towards the west: the rising wind and sea deterred their attempt to move to the east directly into the teeth of the storm. As the Italians moved to the west the British followed, always keeping the smokescreen between the Italians and the convoy and making repeated lunges from the smokescreen against the enemy battle line with gunfire and torpedoes. This forced the Italians to turn away repeatedly. Ultimately the Italians broke off action and retired for their bases, two of their destroyers floundering en route. The battle was an almost perfect example of the importance of 'the weather gauge' (almost unknown since the days of sail) in the course of the action, but also of the effectiveness of an inferior but aggressive force, skilfully handled as an entire formation, beating off a superior enemy. (The similar tactics of standing between convoy and enemy with inferior forces was also successfully employed by the British in the action with the *Scharnhorst* on December 26 1943. After having frustrated several attempts by the *Scharnhorst* to work her way around the flank of the British cruisers, the latter trailed the German battlecruiser to the south after she had broken off the action in order to bring her to a rendezvous with the battleship *Duke of York.* In a classic night-time action involving co-ordinated attack by gun and torpedoes from destroyers, the German ship was destroyed.) At Sirte, however, the Italians did have some compensation for the action delayed the arrival of the convoy at Malta with the result that two of the merchantmen were sunk by aircraft the following day: had there been no delay then almost certainly these ships would have survived.

In a sense this was exactly the same result as the Germans had achieved with the *Tirpitz*, by her very presence in Norwegian waters, against convoy PQ 17. In one of the most disastrous episodes in British naval history, this convoy was ordered to scatter by the Admiralty and the escorts withdrawn in the mistaken belief that they were shortly to be attacked by overwhelming force. The result was that the hapless merchantmen were picked off individually by submarines and aircraft, only thirteen surviving from an original convoy of thirty-six. This was another superb example of the tactical value of a fleet in being and the effect its presence could have on a superior enemy's dispositions.

Neervtheless with the Allied victories in the battles of the sea lanes in the Atlantic and Mediterranean by

mid-1943, the way was clear for Allied sea power to perform another of its vital tasks – putting an army ashore on an enemy coast and supporting its actions against an enemy field army. Five major seaborne landings were made after May 1943 by the Allies – Sicily (July 1943), the Italian mainland (September 1943), Anzio (January 1944), Normandy (June 1944) and the south of France (August 1944). With the exception of Anzio, which was a deliberate attempt to turn a fixed enemy position further to the south, these invasions were direct assaults on an enemy coast, the techniques being gradually and carefully evolved to ensure success. Though Sicily was the largest of the invasions (seven divisions being used), Normandy is generally considered to be the classic of its kind.

Few people realize the extent to which the Allied decision to land in Normandy, as opposed to the Pas de Calais, was determined by purely naval considerations. The strategic choice was limited by the need to provide searoom for the 1213 warships and the 2470 landing ships and landing craft allocated to the assault phase (plus 1656 other landing ships for support operations and the subsequent convoys needed to put more troops ashore and supply the armies once they were established on the continent). Only in the area to the south of the Isle of Wight in the English Channel was there sufficient room to form up such an armada and to allow the feeding in of forces from the small ports on either flank of the Southampton-Portsmouth area. The Straits of Dover were too narrow, the ports in Devon and Cornwall too far away for ships to make an

Below: HMS *Warspite* **shells German positions in Normandy during the D-Day landings in June 1944. Naval firepower was an important part of the Allied success in Normandy. Right: Protected by barrage balloons and the guns of the fleet, Allied forces land from LCT's beached in Normandy. Far Right: Soldiers crammed in LCP's start the run in past a cruiser to land on their beaches.**

undetected night passage to the other end of the Channel, and the ports of south-east England were too small to take an invasion force for the shorter, more direct sea route. The timing of the assault was also determined by naval considerations. Accurate pilotage and the needs of naval gunnery necessitated a daylight assault and hence moonlit passage; daylight was also needed to allow the engineers to clear the beach obstacles. The obstacles themselves demanded that the invasion take place on a rising tide on a day when two high tides in daylight occurred in order to allow the follow up forces to be moved ashore. These considerations meant that an invasion had to take place some forty minutes after dawn and four hours before high tide: such conditions, when combined with moon phase, only occurred on three or four days in a month – a good example of the manner in which natural factors affect naval and military strategy.

In Operation Neptune, the naval side of the Normandy invasion, the emphasis was placed on massive firepower to subdue the enemy (assisted of course by heavy bomber raids that could deliver far more weight of explosive but not so accurately as naval gunfire) during the actual invasion phase. This proved to be of vital importance, particularly on Omaha beach where the Americans lost much of their artillery to the sea and where uncleared obstacles prevented reinforcements getting into action. Direct naval gunfire was critical in suppressing enemy gunfire and in breaking up counter-attacks – just as the *Warspite* had broken up German counter-moves at Salerno and German counter-attacks at Anzio had not been facilitated by some 20,000 rounds fired at them by Allied cruisers and destroyers. This firepower was vital in allowing the armies to get ashore, reorganize and then fight their way inland beyond the range of the guns. Thereafter, the navies' task remained as it had always been, namely the continued supply of the armies in their operations against the enemy field forces. Indeed that the Allied armies liberated France and drove deep into Germany to contribute to the forcing of the Nazi surrender, liberating as a result the Benelux countries, Denmark and Norway, was a sign of the total victory obtained by Anglo-American sea and air forces in the struggle. Without victory on the convoy routes, the British would have been forced to surrender: the Americans might well then have been helpless to affect the European situation. Sea power was the basis of the Allied victories in the west.

The Pacific War

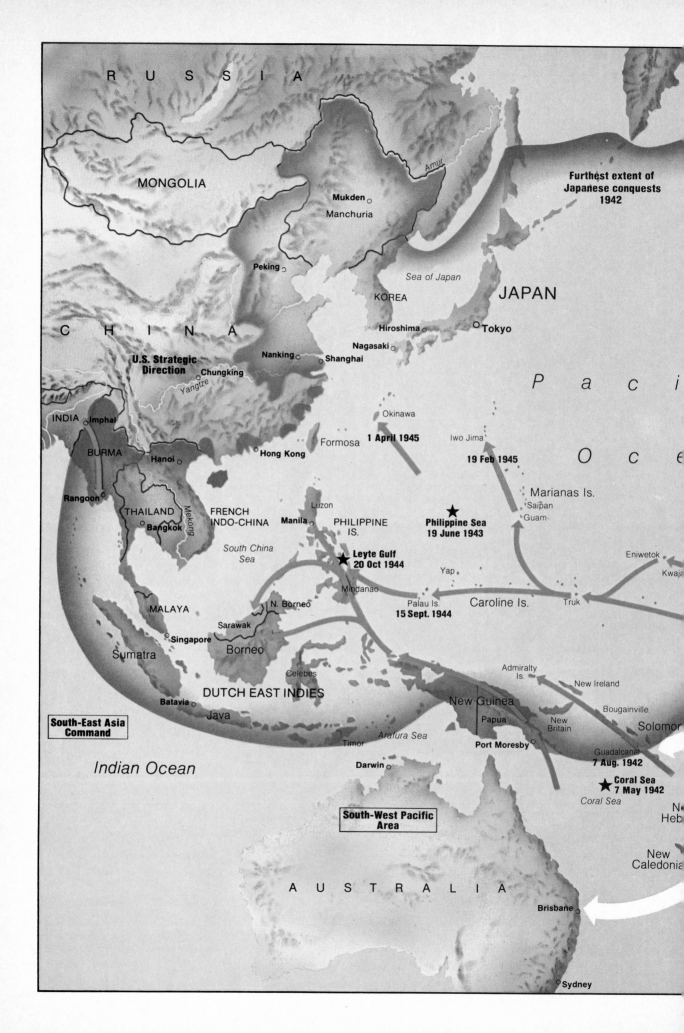

RUSSIA

MONGOLIA

Mukden
Manchuria

Amur

Peking

CHINA

**U.S. Strategic
Direction**

Nanking
Shanghai
Chungking

Yangtze

KOREA

Sea of Japan

JAPAN

Hiroshima
Nagasaki

Tokyo

**Furthest extent of
Japanese conquests
1942**

INDIA
Imphal

BURMA

Hanoi

Rangoon

THAILAND
Bangkok

Mekong

FRENCH
INDO-CHINA

Hong Kong

Formosa

Okinawa

1 April 1945

Iwo Jima

19 Feb 1945

P a c i

O c e

Luzon

Manila

PHILIPPINE
IS.

★
**Philippine Sea
19 June 1943**

Marianas Is.
Saipan
Guam

*South China
Sea*

★ **Leyte Gulf
20 Oct 1944**

Mindanao

Yap

MALAYA

N. Borneo

Sarawak

Singapore

Borneo

Palau Is.
15 Sept. 1944

Caroline Is.

Truk

Eniwetok

Kwaja

Sumatra

Celebes

DUTCH EAST INDIES

Batavia
Java

**South-East Asia
Command**

Indian Ocean

Timor

Darwin

Admiralty
Is.

New Ireland

New Guinea

Papua

New
Britain

Bougainville

Solomon

Arafura Sea

Port Moresby

Guadalcanal
7 Aug. 1942

**South-West Pacific
Area**

★ **Coral Sea
7 May 1942**

Coral Sea

Ne
Heb

New
Caledonia

A U S T R A L I A

Brisbane

Sydney

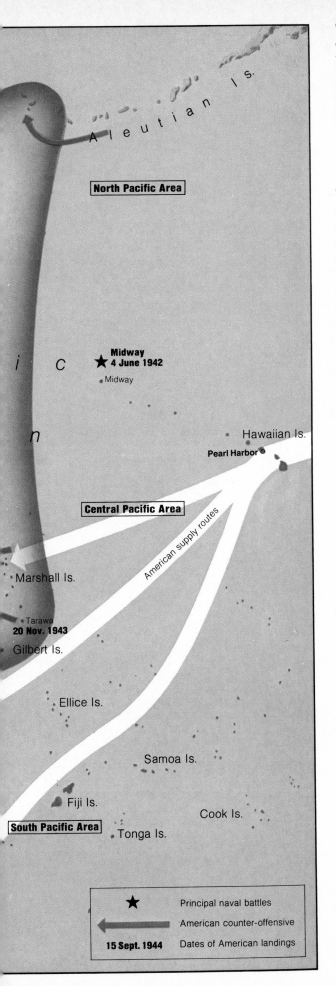

North Pacific Area

★ Midway
4 June 1942

• Midway

Central Pacific Area

American supply routes

Hawaiian Is.

Pearl Harbor

• Marshall Is.

• Tarawa
20 Nov. 1943
Gilbert Is.

• Ellice Is.

Samoa Is.

Fiji Is.

Cook Is.

South Pacific Area

• Tonga Is.

★   Principal naval battles

←   American counter-offensive

15 Sept. 1944   Dates of American landings

The Japanese spoke of a Victory Disease when they described the vast areas of the Pacific and Far East that they had captured during their first blitzkrieg. The strains on their manpower and resources retaining these areas was one of the factors that led to their defeat.

The war in the Pacific is often seen in terms of the great carrier engagements – the Coral Sea and Midway (1942), the Philippine Sea and Leyte Gulf (1944) – that marked the utter and total destruction of the finest fleet in the world in 1941, the Imperial Japanese Navy. In the course of this destruction, the US Navy increased in size and quality to become utterly unchallenged in power and effectiveness. Less well documented is the war that began immediately after Pearl Harbor whereby the Americans, temporarily paralyzed by the losses sustained in the attack, began unrestricted submarine warfare against Japanese commerce. Ultimately this campaign was to prove of immense strategic importance since in effect the Americans imposed an economic blockade on Japan that became a stranglehold. In the course of the war Japan lost 90 per cent of her merchant fleet and, by the time the atomic bombs brought her to surrender, she was economically, industrially and financially exhausted. Totally dependent on seaborne trade for the import of raw materials and the transport of men and materiel to the theatres of war, the Japanese were fatally vulnerable to commerce warfare in the same way as the British. And trade and the transport of resources were totally annihilated in the course of the war. Such was the power of the Japanese Navy, however, that it was not until after 1943 that losses exceeded replacements and that merchant ships were forced to go into areas controlled by American aircraft in order to supply their threatened or beleaguered garrisons. The most spectacular phase of the commerce war was at the end, when US naval air power roamed the skies around Japan and her approaches, destroying the few remaining merchantmen at will. But the real damage lay in the steady rate of attrition inflicted by American submariners throughout the war on the Japanese merchant fleet: 57 per cent of all losses were inflicted by US submarines. The American strategic blockade of Japan was one of the most decisive examples of economic warfare waged by aggressive sea power.

In the course of this war the Americans used their submarines in exactly the same way as the Germans – in hunting packs that closely co-ordinated their efforts to increase their effectiveness. The Americans had great technical superiority over the Japanese in terms of radar and communications: they were also presented with a supreme opportunity because of Japanese neglect of their trade. With the Japanese Navy committed to fleet action, and training geared to that eventuality, the unglamorous defensive nature of convoy protection was initially scorned. The Japanese patrolled the sea lanes in the same manner that the British had before 1917, achieving next to nothing, and shipping was not concentrated but left to sail independently. When, belatedly, the Japanese switched to convoy they afforded protection on a scale totally inadequate to deal with the aggressiveness of the attack; sometimes the escort was as weak as one escort for five to ten merchantmen. And this against American submariners who were prepared to stay at periscope depth and take on escorts with a spread of torpedoes in order to eliminate them and get at the helpless merchantmen.

The Japanese, on the other hand, did not use their submarines in the same manner against the massive American logistics train that stretched across the Pacific. Perhaps naturally, given the overall and growing American superiority of warship numbers, they used their submarines in an effort to write down US naval strength, as the Germans had in World War I. While this policy had some isolated successes – such as the sinking of the *Yorktown* at Midway – it never had any real chance of altering the balance of power. Moreover, such a policy forced the Japanese to attack the most heavily defended part of the American effort at sea and, as a result, their submarines took heavy losses. They would have been well advised to have concentrated on the merchantmen, effecting an even greater dispersal of American striking power than was in fact the case.

After Pearl Harbor the Americans were to a large

Below: Smoke streams from the USS *Yorktown* as she swings hard to port during Japanese air attacks in the Battle of Midway in June 1942. Inset: A Japanese submarine. Despite having the excellent 'long lance' torpedo, the Japanese failed to use their submarines as aggressively as the Americans.

Damage control teams at work on the flight deck of
the USS *Yorktown* after Japanese attacks on June 4,
1942 during the Battle of Midway. American carriers
did not have armoured flight decks which made them
vulnerable to air attack, though this did save weight
and therefore increase speed.

extent the prisoners of circumstances, both strategically and tactically. Strategically, they had to stand on the defence, for they lacked the strength to contest the Japanese conquest of South-East Asia. To the Americans, the defence of the island chain from Hawaii to Midway, and the sea routes to Australia and New Zealand, were paramount. Tactically, Pearl Harbor had shown that the torpedo and the bomb were the decisive weapons of naval warfare, that carriers could deliver massive and strategically decisive blows in their own right – even though the Japanese actually failed to achieve decisive success at Pearl Harbor since they missed the carriers, dockyard and oil storage depot. (Had they been destroyed, it is difficult to see how the Americans could have avoided withdrawing the remaining fleet to California, with incalculable results.)

Because of the absence of an effective battle line the only means of active defence for the Americans after Pearl Harbor was bound to be centred on the carrier. They basically evolved the notion of the fast carrier striking force, a carrier or carriers operating with a close cruiser and destroyer escort. Such forces operated in semi-independent groups whose movements were co-ordinated to give mutual support and concentrated offensive power where possible. In the early stages of the war a carrier group, if it contained more than one carrier, divided in order to launch or recover its aircraft: at Midway Task Force 16 divided into two groups, one centred on the *Hornet*, the other on the *Enterprise*. By 1943, however, task forces stopped dividing and stayed together under all circumstances in order to increase the effectiveness and strength of the continuous Combat Air Patrols (CAP) and the fire-power that could be put up by the escorts against enemy aircraft. By 1944, the Japanese use of suicide aircraft against American naval ships – one in four caused some damage and one in thirty-three sank a ship – forced further changes in the tactical deployment of the carrier forces.

In December 1944 the new tactics were employed for the first time in support of operations against Mindoro in the Philippines. Task Force 38 was divided into three groups: TF 38.1, with two fleet carriers, two light carriers, two battleships, three heavy and one anti-aircraft cruisers, and eighteen destroyers, was the weakest of the three and only a little weaker than the whole of the force that the Americans had deployed at Midway. In order to give advanced warning of suicide attacks advanced destroyer pickets were

posted some sixty miles before the fleet, and equipped with modern radar and homing devices. American aircraft returning to the carriers were obliged to 'report' to the pickets and circle them, thereby allowing any Japanese aircraft that attempted to join the stream to be identified and eliminated. These pickets, which were under the CAP, were posted wide in order to leave a clear passage for Japanese aircraft, and an uncluttered radar picture for the fleet itself. In addition, the Americans altered the balance of aircraft on their carriers. Formerly an *Essex* class carrier on average carried thirty-eight fighters, thirty-six dive bombers and fifteen torpedo-carrying aircraft; after December 1944 such carriers had seventy-three fighters, fifteen bombers and fifteen torpedo planes – a far superior defensive capability than had previously existed, but also an increase in offensive power since the change in

balance was accompanied by modifications to the *Hellcat* and *Corsair* fighters that effectively made them general-purpose aircraft. With a 2000-lb bomb load and a capacity for unescorted bombing operations, such fighters in fact doubled the striking power of the carriers.

For the Mindoro operation the Americans employed a tactic known as the Big Blue Blanket, which was effectively a Day and Night CAP not over the fleet but over the enemy's airfields. When fighters were due for relief, bombers took over to keep the airfields neutralized. For Mindoro, the Americans flew 1671 sorties (1427 of them by fighters) over the Japanese airfields on Luzon, with the result that the invasion forces went untouched by Japanese aircraft based there: overall the balance of losses during these operations decisively favoured the Americans.

The USS *Enterprise* about to launch Douglas Dauntless fighters on May 4, 1942 during the Battle of the Coral Sea.

Such were the major tactics adopted by the Americans in the heady days of 1944-45 as their forces triumphantly swept across the western Pacific, taking losses of men, aircraft and ships but at a cost totally exorbitant to the Japanese. American strategy, so tentative and defensive in the dark days after Pearl Harbor, had been able to contest Japanese control of the central Pacific in June 1942, when the latter attempted to complete the task bungled the year before at Pearl Harbor. In attacking towards Midway, the Japanese had hoped to secure their defensive perimeter and possibly bring American carriers to battle, but it was the latter that secured victory. Fighting defensively and trying to keep at maximum distance from the Japanese, the Americans had the supreme advantage that they had broken the Japanese naval codes: they were able to catch the divided Japanese forces and,

concentrating against the carriers, were able to sink four of them for the loss of the *Yorktown*. Most of the Japanese carriers were lost when they were caught in the process of re-arming and refuelling their aircraft on the decks by a providential coincidence of a torpedo-plane and dive-bomber assault – just as the text book had always stressed, but in this case somewhat fortuitous in its timing. As a result of this battle a rough balance of forces in the central Pacific came into existence.

With the defeat of the Japanese in the central Pacific and the earlier checking of the Japanese southern thrust at the Battle of the Coral Sea, the Americans were actively able to contest the Japanese advance in the Solomons by landing on Guadalcanal on August 7 1942. Japanese resistance on the island ended in February 1943 when they evacuated their remaining forces and cut their losses. The landings on Guadalcanal were made to deny the Japanese a forward air base and the possession of this air base brought about a series of naval battles in the seas around the Solomons that were of immense strategic and tactical importance.

In the early exchanges, the sheer professionalism and expertise of the Japanese, particularly in night fighting and torpedo attacks from both cruisers and destroyers, provided them with a decisive superiority over the Americans, even though the latter had radar. The Japanese were also able to achieve a tactical success at the Battle of Santa Cruz where the Americans lost the *Hornet*. Over time however the Japanese, for all their fighting qualities, could not stand up to the sheer volume of the American resources being fed into the battle when this was combined with a more effective use of radar and growing battle experience. Though worsted in many of the engagements, the Americans achieved decisive strategic success at Guadalcanal and inflicted losses that the Japanese could ill-afford.

The slackening of the Japanese impetus and the steady accumulation of American strength, allowed the Americans to assume an offensive that became increasingly dynamic and imaginative with the passing of time. Their strategy essentially involved the by-passing of resistance where possible, leaving the strength of the Japanese to wither like a severed limb. The process, known as 'island-hopping', basically went for the gaps attempting to seize islands from which aircraft could operate. Nevertheless this policy involved the Americans in many severe actions, costly in blood and effort, against an enemy that until almost the end of the war fought to the last man. Yet few campaigns better illustrate the great flexibility of sea power than the American drive across the western Pacific in 1944. Starting from their secured positions in the Solomons and the Gilberts, they drove through the Marshalls to the Marianas (by-passing the scattered Carolines) – an 800-mile jump. At the same time, they conducted a series of landings along the Papuan coast and thrust towards the Philippines. The policy of switching the point of attack along two separate axes of advance, with the choice of timing and target, enabled them to put the Japanese on the horns of a dilemma: as the threat from

the Solomons developed, the Japanese were im mobilized in 'no-man's land' at Truk, unable to mov against the American strength in the Gilberts becaus of the developments on their right flank. Only when th Americans assaulted Saipan did the Japanese come ou to give battle in the Philippine Sea and here their pain fully rebuilt carrier forces were annihilated in a cautiou defensive action. Though severely criticized at th time, the defensive tactics of the Americans allowec them to concentrate their fighters for battle over th American fleet and by destroying Japanese carrier air craft they destroyed the effectiveness of the carriers a effectively as if the carriers themselves had been sunk In all, the Japanese lost three carriers (two to sub marines) and had two more heavily damaged: over 40c irreplaceable aircraft and their crews were lost. Th Japanese Navy was ruined in the Battle of the Philip pine Sea for even though many battleships and lighter surface ships remained, they were of small account Victory paved the way for the American invasion of the Philippines where, again, the Japanese were forced tc give battle. In this battle, the Japanese deliberately divided their forces and used their empty carriers as bait to draw away American carrier forces in order that their surface ships could get among the invasion force. The plan almost worked but in the end the Battle of Leyte Gulf showed that the Japanese were virtually at the end of their tether. With the invasion in 1945 of Iwo Jima and then Okinawa, the way was clear for a concerted air attack on the Japanese home islands themselves: the air bombardment was joined in July by the first ship bombardments – an indication in itself of the totality of US naval and air power.

Total sea supremacy had been obtained by the Americans by the time the Japanese were brought to surrender. It was indeed appropriate that the signing of the instrument of surrender should take place in Tokyo Bay aboard a US Navy ship, for it had been sea power that had decided the issue in the Pacific. Yet by an irony the surrender was signed aboard the battleship *Missouri*, of all the types of ship involved in securing the American victory, perhaps the least important. In some ways, however, the choice of the *Missouri* was perhaps pertinent after all, for the surrender marked the end of an era, the end of the line for the battleship. No longer would such ships play a major part in war at sea: Tokyo Bay marked the passing of the ship that had been synonymous with sea power itself for over 300 years.

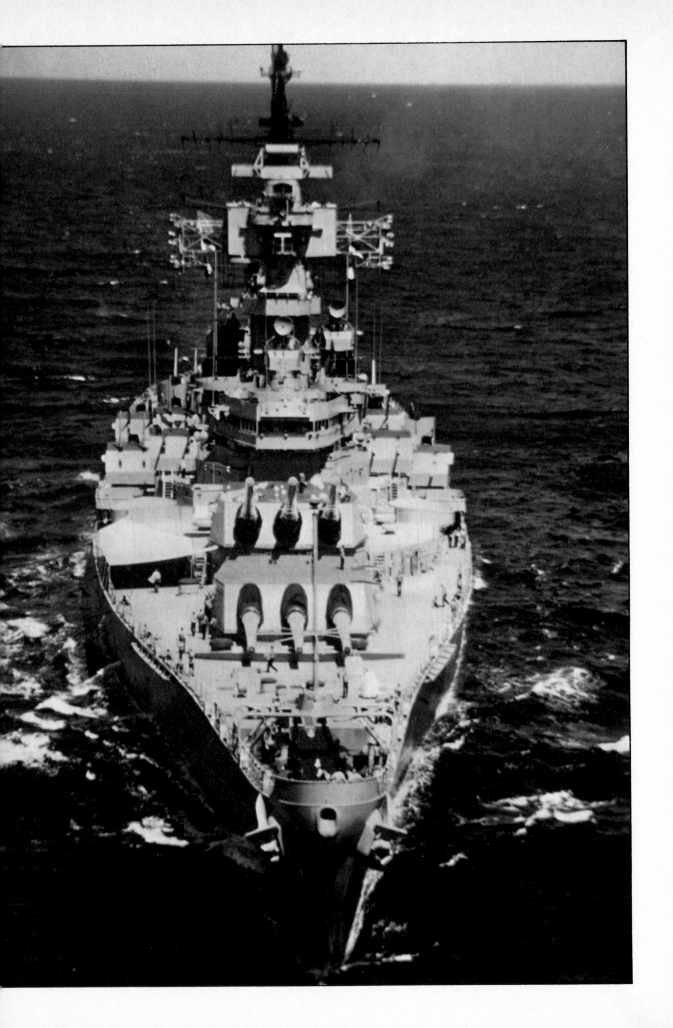

Sea Power
in the Nuclear Age

The defeat of the Axis powers in 1945 in no way lessened the importance of sea power: it provided, in fact, the basis for many of the Western Allies' subsequent actions – the surrender of the former enemies (most notably Japan) and the reduction and repatriation of the American and British armies overseas to name only two. The disarming and repatriation of the defeated enemies, the despatch of armies of occupation (as in China and Japan), the shipment home of prisoners of war and demobilized soldiers, the imposition of order in certain areas (such as Greece) and the sending of urgently needed supplies and aid to liberated territories were also actions only made possible by the immense naval power of the Western democracies. For years after the war clearance of the debris of war – the removal of wrecks, and the clearing and destruction of mines and bombs – were also tasks that required considerable efforts on the part of naval forces.

The basis for such actions was American naval power. Following the sun's path from the Elbe to Vladivostock ran the writ of the American Navy; nothing on the surface of the seas could move except by her permission. Strong though her forces on land and in the air were, the backbone of American strength was her incomparable Navy beside which even the Royal Navy was dwarfed into insignificance. Local areas of control and influence remained to the British but British naval power was a complement and not a rival to or independent of US naval strength. For the reality of the situation was that an impoverished Britain, dependent on the Americans for almost all her escort carriers and many of her high performance aircraft, could not maintain her position. In the disastrous winter of 1947 the commissioned strength of the Royal Navy in home waters was reduced to one cruiser and three destroyers: the rest were being scrapped, held in reserve or were being used as training ships. The Pax Britannica had indeed passed, and control of the seas had been assumed by stronger friendly hands.

The advent of the nuclear age did not initially affect navies a great deal. The 1946 nuclear tests by the Americans at Bikini Atoll in the Pacific demonstrated the vulnerability of warships to direct or close nuclear attack, but the wisdom of the time decreed that for the most part nuclear attack would not wreak too much damage on a reasonably dispersed naval force and that, in any case, the paucity of nuclear weapons for the next few years would probably mean that any likely enemy (i.e. the Soviet Union) would be far more likely to use nuclear weapons against the homeland and against naval bases than against a fleet at sea. The development of nuclear weapons, therefore, had little effect on tactics. Moreover, strategically, navies were not immediately concerned with them because they were incapable of delivering them. The great size and weight of nuclear weapons, and the need to have heavy aircraft in order to lift them, meant that naval aircraft and, more importantly, aircraft carriers, were utterly unsuited to deliver them. This did not mean that the US Navy did not want to have a nuclear capability and did not fight hard to secure one, but it did lose the initial contest for the control of such weapons to the newly formed US Air Force, even though at the time, only the heavy strategic bombers of the latter were able to deliver nuclear weapons on their targets. So the strategic role of the navies – particularly the US Navy – remained conventional.

The fleets were a powerful weapon of diplomacy, capable of demonstrating a nation's interests, influence and determination. They could be used to exert pressure, without necessarily crossing a threshold of violence in some crisis situation. For the British and French, the need for, and importance of, sea power in colonial operations was quickly shown as their respective empires were quickly involved in countering insurgency in various areas. The French ability to re-establish their position in Indo-China by transportation of troops to that area, to give close fire support to coastal operations, to launch riverine operations and to patrol coastal waters to prevent infiltration or insurgent operations, all depended on sea power. In part the failure of insurgency movements in Malaya and the Philippines can be traced not only to their isolation from external sources of support and supply by the sea but also to the naval might of the British in the first instance and the reality, if distant, of American sea power in the second. Later the Korean and Vietnam Wars were to demonstrate the vital importance of sea power in conventional conflict fought under the nuclear umbrella. During the Korean War it was US sea power that saved South Korea from communist aggression. The desperate position of the United Nations forces in the Pusan perimeter was held only because of the massive contribution of US sea power – when the UN forces were virtually at the end of their tether and confronted by a strong and aggressive enemy, the defence and reinforcement of Pusan was achieved by the US Navy, particularly in the form of naval gun

The USS *New Jersey* bombards Communist-held territory near Wonsan in Korea. Carriers made battleships too vulnerable and too expensive to operate, and the *New Jersey* is now no longer active.

support and close air support. In all naval ships fired some 4 million shells and naval aircraft flew over 250,000 sorties in the course of the Korean War. Important though these contributions were, they somewhat pale into insignificance when set against the sheer audacity and inspired brilliance of the Inchon landing of September 1950. While still in contact with a superior and attacking enemy, the Americans divided their forces to launch an amphibious attack against the communist flank where the combination of sea to the west and mountains to the east forced the enemy lines of communication through a narrow, restricted gap. Attacking defended position in waters where some of their craft drew less than one foot of water under their keels, the Americans fought their way ashore and then inland to stand across the communist line of retreat, thus bringing about a massive battle of encirclement and annihilation that was almost total in its extent. In subsequent operations the naval forces performed vital tasks in the recovery of ditched aircrews, the patrolling of the coasts and in evacuating United Nations forces from Korea. Later, in Vietnam, the great strength and invulnerability of sea power was most clearly shown as US naval forces pounded communist positions both north and south of the 17th Parallel. The losses that US aircraft took on the ground to night-time communist rocket and gun attack was in marked contrast to the invulnerability of aircraft far out to sea on the decks and in the hangars of the carriers. Flexibility, invulnerability and immense destructive power were clearly revealed by such operations.

Sea power, therefore, was of immense importance in such circumstances as 'limited wars'. It was also critical in demonstrating power, interest and intention in a crisis situation. The appeal for American intervention by the Lebanese authorities in 1958 was only met because the US Navy could send marines ashore and aircraft overhead almost immediately; the imposition of quarantine on Cuba in 1962 as the means of forcing the USSR to conform to US wishes was possible only because America at that time enjoyed almost total supremacy in the western Atlantic. The quarantine enabled the Americans to make an overt political and diplomatic move that provided time for the opposition to reflect on the options open without the immediate pressure of direct military confrontation that would have been present in a situation where land forces were mobilized. The invasion of the Dominican Republic in 1965 was a naval operation, an immediate and flexible response to a situation in which the Americans felt that vital US interests (and credibility throughout Latin America) was at stake.

Although the South Koreans' position was secure, mainly as a result of US sea power, it must also be noted that the Korean conflict went a long way to restoring American naval power, for by the time the Korean War broke out the US Navy had declined to a seven carrier fleet with hundreds of ships either stricken or in reserve, and with almost no new construction in hand. Virtually the only exception to this near halt in construction was the building of the massive *Midway* class carriers which had two novel features – they were the first American carriers to incorporate armoured flight decks, the value of which had been amply demonstrated by British carriers during the latter stages of the Pacific war and they were also the first American warships incapable of passing through the Panama Canal. In this they relinquished strategic flexibility for the tactical and technological requirements of broad beam and extra displacement.

The Korean War reconvinced the Americans of the need for strong carrier forces and indeed by the end of the war eighteen carriers had served off Korea, of which sixteen were kept in commission for many years after the war had ended. Technological developments

63

The cutting edge of a carrier: a US Navy Phantom laden with missiles, weapons pads and fuel tanks at the moment of take-off. Right: A British Hawker Siddeley Harrier VTOL fighter bomber during trials on HMS *Ark Royal* off Portland.

necessitated the construction of new classes of carriers after 1950: the *Forrestal*, laid down in 1952, needed longer flight decks than had previously been incorporated into carriers, in order to handle the new generation of jet aircraft. She was also given an enclosed prow to improve her seaworthiness, and during construction she was modified to incorporate three British inventions – the angled flight deck, steam catapults and the mirror landing aid. The angled flight deck was a major step forward since it allowed the simultaneous despatch and recovery of aircraft with comparative safety. The *Forrestal* and her three sister ships were followed by two ships of the *Kitty Hawk* class and then the *Enterprise*. With the building of the latter, the sheer cost of such ships began to make itself felt – the nuclear powered *Enterprise* cost $451 millions compared to the $265 millions of the *Kitty Hawk* class (the *Midway* class cost $81 millions) – and this caused a reversion to conventional power in the *John F. Kennedy* class ($280 millions), even though the nuclear propul-

sion of the *Enterprise* gave her immensely high speed and long-range endurance. On her original cores the *Enterprise* steamed 200,000 miles in her first three years, though her great flexibility was somewhat limited by the fact that most of her escorts were conventional. The limitation imposed upon capability by rising costs can be gauged by the fact that the US Navy is now a thirteen carrier force since the cost of replacing the older carriers is now very nearly prohibitive. The *Nimitz*, commissioned in May 1975, initially cost $1881 millions and her two sister ships, the *Dwight D Eisenhower* and the *Carl Vinson*, are confidently expected to break the $2 billion ceiling. The staggering cost – an eleven-fold increase in twenty-five years – has effectively put the acquisition of such ships beyond the reach of the Europeans, even without considering the difficulties they would have in finding the 6300 men needed to man a ship such as the *Nimitz*. Such costs may soon prove to be beyond the reach of Americans themselves. In order to seek a way around the problem

in 1975, the American Navy sought approval for a 14,300 ton ship of an escort type known as a Sea Control Ship (SCS) armed with three VSTOL aircraft and sixteen helicopters, many of the characteristics approximating those of the British *Invincible* (launched May 1977). The US Congress, however, threw out the request on the grounds that the ships were too small, too slow and lacked offensive capability, even though trials on the *USS Guam* in a SCS role between 1972 and 1974 had proved satisfactory. The result has been that the US Navy has made proposals for a new class of 'light' carrier, something between 40,000 and 50,000 tons or similar to the *Ark Royal*, that could operate fixed wing VSTOL aircraft. Such ships would be suited to sea control operations (that is, securing control of the seas surrounding the areas in which the ship operated), supporting amphibious operations and providing close air support, conducting mine warfare and for operations in which her aircraft would not be involved in a direct fight for air supremacy. Although her

aircraft could be used to deal with reconnaissance aircraft and bombers, they would not be equipped to fight high-performance fighters or attack aircraft – that task would remain the role of the fleet carriers with whom the light carriers could keep pace.

It is precisely in this increasingly costly field of carrier aviation that the Western navies still retain their most decisive advantage over the Soviet Navy at the present time. In the fifties, at the time of Korea and the building of the *Forrestal*, the US Navy emerged from the shadows of the US Air Force and secured for the carriers a major nuclear role. The miniaturization of nuclear weapons and the development of long-range jet aircraft capable of operating off a carrier deck allowed the Navy to emerge, not as a competitor, but as a complement to the Air Force as the means of delivering nuclear weapons. Moreover, they had one great advantage over the Strategic Air Command in this role in that the carriers, unlike airfields, were mobile and could pose immense problems of detection and destruction

HMS *Fearless* **an assault landing ship with a self-flooding dock area aft. Not only can she launch and recover landing craft, her dock area has a deck which serves as a landing pad for Wessex helicopters. She is equipped to serve as an off-shore HQ for a joint naval and land task force.**

for the defender. Nevertheless, the role of the US carriers as a major part of the strategic nuclear deterrent was relatively short-lived. The development of other means of delivery meant that the carriers, though important, became somewhat downgraded in the purely nuclear sense.

By the early sixties, particularly with Vietnam beginning to make itself felt, the role of the carriers in limited warfare operations began to become more important at the expense of the nuclear role. Today the carrier still has a nuclear role but the overwhelming part of its *raison d'etre* remains its conventional capability. Any amphibious landing or seaborne reinforcement of a threatened area – such as the northern flank in the event of a war with the Soviet Union – would have to be made under the protective umbrella of carrier aircraft: major reinforcements of the European theatre by the Americans could involve carriers, granted the strength and range of the latest Soviet naval aircraft. Support for land forces in contact with the enemy would also have to be made under air cover. In this role the carrier is absolutely vital and the task forces formed to discharge such tasks would have to be formed around the carrier. Such task forces besides the carrier(s) would have to include solid- and liquid-replenishment ships, and naval vessels armed with weapons capable of protecting not only the individual ship but the force as a whole. A task force would have to be screened, particularly to the fore, by anti-submarine warfare ships, whose sonar searches overlapped: these would probably be preceded by their helicopters working in front searching for submarines or surface ships of the enemy. In immediate support of the carriers would have to be the heavier of the escorts that were capable of dealing with submerged or missile attack and, most importantly, some anti-aircraft capability to supplement the carriers own Combat Air Patrols. The CAPs would probably be well forward of the task force, perhaps some sixty to eighty miles in advance, in order to give as much warning as possible of the approach of hostile aircraft. Given the existence of stand-off weapons, carrier aircraft would have to think in terms of intercepting and destroying enemy bomber forces several hundred miles before the task force, rather than relying on the missiles of the task force to deal with the enemy weapons. (The task force could also be scouted by patrol lines of conventional submarines and hunter-killer submarines).

The carriers were the first means by which the US

Navy secured a nuclear role. In 1954, however, the US Navy launched the first nuclear propelled submarine, the *USS Nautilus*, a patrol submarine armed with conventional torpedoes. Nuclear propulsion enabled the submarine to become a proper submarine craft rather than a ship that could submerge; it also gave great underwater speed and endurance and hence invulnerability from surface ships. (In one of her earliest voyages the *Nautilus* sailed nearly 1400 miles at 20 knots

submerged.) The logic of nuclear deterrence pointed the way to a further dispersal of the means of delivery by evolving a nuclear-powered submarine armed with strategic nuclear missiles. The first US submarine to carry nuclear missiles was the *Halibut*, initially designed with conventional power. At first the *Halibut* and her sisters were armed with the 575-mile range *Regulus I* missile that could only be fired from a surfaced submarine; this, combined with the limited range

of the missile, meant that the submarines were vulnerable to detection and destruction since they had to come quite close to their targets and show themselves. The only solution to the tactical problems thus caused was the evolution of longer-range missiles that could be fired underwater; indeed, the *Halibut* and her sisters were intended only as an interim measure until such weapons were available. The first occasion on which a submarine (the *George Washington*) fired a strategic

HMS *Ark Royal* **and the USS** *Forrestal* **during joint naval exercises in July 1976. Conventional carriers like these will in time be replaced by 'through deck' versions.**

missile while submerged was on July 20, 1960, the missile being the 1200-mile range *Polaris A-1*. The role of the submarine as the most effective means of delivering strategic nuclear weapons on account of

The Soviet tank landing ship *Ropucha* in the Englis▮
Channel, photographed by a Sea King from HM▮
Blake. NATO and Warsaw Pact navies photograph an▮
monitor the movements of each others fleets.

her endurance, mobility and comparative invulnerability has grown from this time, though only at the
expense of developing longer-ranged missiles and larger
submarines capable of carrying them. The initial
Polaris submarines, costing about $100 millions, were
subsequently replaced by longer-ranged Marks of the
Polaris and then by submarines armed with the 2800-
mile *Poseidon* missile. The *Poseidon* in its turn will be
replaced by the 4000-mile range *Titan*, with a 6000
Mark II projected. The cost of new submarines capable of delivering such weapons is enormous: in 1977
the US Navy programmed $1969 millions for just two.

Such escalating costs – roughly parallel to the rising
cost of the carriers – have to be borne by the Americans
in order to hold diplomatic cards in the Strategic Arms
Limitation Talks (SALT) and to maintain the whole
credibility of the American nuclear deterrent upon
which the security of both the United States and NATO
depends. The *Titan* missiles are almost literally inter-
continental in their range: without moving from their
West Coast base they can hit virtually any major city in
China or the Soviet Union. No time need therefore be
lost in moving to and from patrol areas, and even greater
areas of ocean will be made available for nuclear submarines to try to hide in – multiplying the difficulties
of the defence and making it harder to take effective
counter-measures. Heavy though the cost may be,
there would seem to be no alternative to such ex-
penditure, granted that the Americans must begin to
replace many of their older nuclear submarines and
that the Soviets already have equivalent submarines
and missiles.

Since the end of World War II one of the more re-
markable developments at sea has been the growth
of the Soviet Navy. For a country that is largely land-
locked, which has very little need for seaborne trade
and which in 1945 had a navy that was virtually ir-
relevant in equipment and wartime performance, the
change from impotence to a position whereby she can
challenge the naval power of the US on an almost
equal footing is most profound. While they still have
many difficulties to face – most notably the physical
separation of forces by the sheer size of the Soviet
homeland – and while there remain certain areas of
Western superiority at sea, the continued growth of the
Soviet Navy, both quantitative and qualitative, is
bound to be of great concern to the West. For while it
was possible to see its development in the forties and
early fifties as a reflex action to Western martitime

supremacy, that supremacy has already passed and
some degree of nuclear parity has now been obtained,
so the continued relentless production of Soviet
warships can hardly be seen in purely defensive terms
or as a defence of marginal maritime interests.

The Soviet Navy, taking its place alongside the
Army, strategic rocket and air defence forces in attempting to fulfill distinct political and strategic objectives, exists for three basic purposes. Initially it
secures the defence of the Soviet Union and the Soviet-
bloc countries. To this end it plays a part in the deployment of the Soviet nuclear deterrent and possesses
forces for operations against American nuclear submarines. It also possesses a capability in conventional

surface and air units that could prevent an orthodox attack from the sea by the West and is also capable of conducting offensive conventional operations on the high seas. As such, it exists in order to 'write down' the conventional power of the Americans, Western Europeans and the Chinese. The third role is the promotion of Soviet interests and the cause of communism (mutually identifiable in Soviet eyes) through such matters as intervention in 'wars of national liberation' – such as Angola. They are also aware, from the way in which naval power has been used by the British and Americans, that a fleet is a powerful instrument of diplomacy, not simply to show the flag and demonstrate power and determination, but also

in a subtle use of force or pressure below a threshold of violence that could lead to wider conflict. Conversely the Soviet presence at sea at the present time means that certain responses that have been available to the West in the past may not now be possible, for arguably the recent build-up of the Soviet fleet must be seen in conjunction with the Soviet build-up in land and air forces and not simply in terms of defence or keeping Eastern Europe in check. One does not need long-range bombers and nuclear submarines to hold Warsaw in line.

The Soviet naval performance in World War II was very poor. This was the result partly of poor training and equipment (particularly with regard to radar and

A Soviet Whiskey Class submarine showing signs of a long stay at sea. Russia has the world's largest submarine fleet, which would give her the ability to wage a crippling campaign against islands such as Britain and Japan in a conventional war.

sonar) and partly because the Soviets, particularly in the early years, were forced to use their sailors in many of the great land battles where their losses were immense. Soviet historians have denigrated the importance of the Anglo-American naval contribution to Allied victories and have claimed considerable successes for their own forces, but the truth of the matter is that the Soviet naval effort in World War II, particularly when it is remembered that in 1941 the Soviets had more submarines than the Germans, was derisory. In only one area did the Soviet Navy perform at all well: their river flotillas, especially when they took part in operations in support of the land forces, as at Stalingrad, were very effective. It is worth noting that Sergei S. Gorshkov, now Commander-in-Chief of the Soviet Navy first came into prominence as commander of the Sea of Azov flotilla during the war.

In the years immediately after World War II the Soviets naturally placed their priorities on national recovery, the needs of the Army and the development of atomic weapons. (Nuclear weapons were secured in 1949; thermo-nuclear weapons after 1953.) Nevertheless, impressive progress was made during this time in expanding the Navy – in itself a major task given the massive destruction of naval bases, construction facilities and ports during the war. Equally importantly, a massive missile research and development programme must have been undertaken during the ten years after the war, given the Soviet Navy's deployment of missiles in the later fifties and early sixties.

Just what they were aiming to achieve during this period is hard to discern. It may be that they were aiming to build a substantial balanced oceanic fleet with carriers, battleships and cruisers with attendant ships, but that this dream never materialized. And it may have been abandoned as a result of the patent inability of Soviet industry to meet all its objectives, or when the realization of the scale of American rearmament after

Korea meant that any such idea of a balanced surface fleet was tantamount to giving the US Navy live target practice in the event of war: there really was little point in building a carrier or two when the Americans had sixteen or more ready for operations. But Stalin was known to favour a big navy and was attracted by the notion of ocean-going ships that could push the defences, interests and capabilities of the USSR even further from the Soviet heartland. On the other hand, however, it would seem that the Soviet Navy was built along more limited, defensive and prudent lines and that their forces were finally built up in order to fulfill three distinct objectives: firstly, to provide sufficient forces to deny the Western navies control of certain waters washing Soviet and Soviet-controlled territories; secondly, the provision of a coastal capability for operations in conjunction with the Army; and, thirdly, an ability to carry out operations on the high seas against Western commerce and American military movements across the Atlantic to Europe. In the immediate post-war period the Soviets concentrated upon completing various ships on which work had stopped because of the war; once these were completed new programmes involving modern vessels were put in hand. Of these new vessels probably the most important were the submarines of the *Whisky* class, seemingly based on the German Type XXI submarine and superior to any submarine then in service with Western navies. Perhaps as many as 230 were built by 1957, and there were some fifty of the less successful *Quebec* and (larger) *Zulu* classes completed by that time. The overall strength of the submarine arm by late 1958 was about 470 – more than the Germans had possessed at any single time between 1939 and 1945. At the same time the Soviets pressed ahead with cruisers and destroyers. Fourteen of the graceful if obsolete *Sverdlov* 6-in cruisers were completed while the powerful *Skoryi* class destroyers were followed by the

An RAF Nimrod banks to port as it circles a Soviet Kotlin Class destroyer near a North Sea oil rig in April 1975. The Russians have an economic as well as strategic interest in the exploration of the North Sea oilfields, and the protection of these resources has become an important priority for NATO, particularly the British and Norwegians.

larger *Kotlin* class.

The death of Stalin seems to have caused some wavering in naval construction, just as it did in the whole Soviet political sphere. The direction of naval policy had certainly entered a new phase by 1956 with the supremacy of Khrushchev within the Soviet political hierarchy and that of Gorshkov as Commander-in-Chief of the Navy. This new regime did inherit certain considerable assets. Firstly, Krushchev's great concern to build up strategic nuclear forces – later to lead to conflict with the military because of the cuts on conventional forces as a result – coincided with the technological developments that made possible submarine-launched strategic missiles. The first tests on ballistic missiles for submarines were carried out in 1955 by the Soviet Union, the same year that the first six *Zulu-V* class submarines began conversion in order to carry 300-mile SS-N-4 *Sark* missiles. It seems that these submarines pre-date the *Halibut* and, in a sense, this was understandable. Given the fact that the Soviets lacked forward bases and long-range bombers, it was natural that missiles and submarine launchers should be of immediate interest to them: the fact that the missiles were of such short range was to the Soviets the spur that the *Regulus* proved to be for the Americans – to implement further development in order to secure invulnerability.

By the time that the *Zulu* conversions were complete, work had already started on new submarines capable of carrying strategic nuclear weapons. Some of these were nuclear-powered, others conventionally fuelled. These were the nuclear *Hotel* and the conventional *Golf* submarines: both classes were initially armed with the *Sark* but then re-equipped with the 700-mile *Serb* missile. By the early sixties the Soviets were building roughly along the same lines as the Americans though slightly behind them: moreover their submarines were neither as good nor as quiet as the American ones. The Soviet equivalent of *Polaris* was the *Yankee* class with sixteen SS-N-6 missiles. These 1300-mile range missiles meant that Soviet submarines could not strike central USA; although this target was subsequently made possible with the development of the *Delta* class with twelve 4200-mile SS-N-8 missiles, which were superior in range and warhead size to any contemporary American naval missile. The acquisition of such missiles enabled the *Delta* class to be effective against the USA even in Arctic waters, without having to enter the Atlantic and

74

A Russian Krupney Class guided missile destroyer.
This type of vessel has gun and missile firepower
vastly superior to destroyers of World War II. She is
armed with a range of surface-to-surface and surface-
to-air missiles as well as anti-submarine rocket launchers, torpedo tubes and radar controlled light
anti-aircraft guns.

Pacific Oceans. (Western sources estimate that the Soviets have some fifty to sixty SSBN submarines, most of which are with the northern fleet based on Sveromorsk.)

The development of SSBN submarines was obviously a major part of Soviet submarine development and was vital to the deployment of their nuclear deterrent, but it was not the only area of development. In addition to the SSBN and the continued construction of conventional patrol submarines (such as the plentiful *Foxtrot* class built after 1958), they developed submarines that were equipped for a hunter-killer role (against Western SSBN submarines) and for operations against Western surface ships by virtue of cruise missiles. The latter type of missile seems to have been built specifically with Western carriers and task forces in mind, possibly intending short- or medium-range missiles (with either conventional or nuclear warheads) to be used in conjunction with an aircraft relay system against surface targets. Such submarines included the *Juliet* class (conventionally-powered) and the nuclear *Echo* class, both of which were commissioned in quite large numbers in the mid-sixties, and which are now mostly deployed with the northern fleet.

Overall at the present time the Soviet Navy deploys about 400 submarines of all types, just over half of which are conventional patrol submarines (of which half of them are of the *Whisky* class). The total capability of this force is impressive not only in its deterrence role but also in the conventional role against trade and military convoys on the oceans. Its importance in the latter role is likely to increase in a situation of Mutually Assured Destruction, particularly if a war did not result in a short nuclear exchange but in a long, drawn-out war of attrition where numbers and not quality were of the essence. The quality of Soviet submarines has definitely improved and the number of nuclear-powered submarines is constantly increasing – although this must be balanced against the decline in the number of older submarines, particularly of the *Whisky*, *Quebec* and *Zulu* classes that must now be approaching the end of their active service lives.

Throughout the Krushchev era, there were important developments in the field of strategic missiles, and his successors have continued the pattern he helped create in his ten years of leadership, by enhancing even further the conventional surface strength of the Navy. The most marked feature of these developments has been the arming of most new ships with missiles.

After the *Sverdlov* class was cut back from twenty-four to fourteen ships, there was an inter-regnum of some six years before the first of *Kynda* class appeared in 1962. The *Kynda* class was seemingly the first purpose-built guided-missile warship: earlier the Soviets had modified certain of their destroyers to take either SS-N or SA-N missiles (in the case of the *Kildins* between 1957 and 1962; with the *Krupnys* after 1960). Much of the missile development was directed to fill the one glaring weakness in the Soviet position at sea – the lack of an organic air defence. The first air defence missile to be fitted in Soviet ships was the SA-N-1 or *Goa* missile, believed to have a 15-mile slant range and a ceiling of 12,000m: subsequently the SA-N-2 (*Guideline*), SA-N-3 (*Goblet*) and SA-N-4 have been introduced, and the latter two are now used very extensively. (The SA-N-4 is believed to be the naval equivalent of the Soviet Army's *Gecko* missile.)

Attention has also been paid to the provision of a considerable punch against surface and submerged enemy ships, the Soviets arming their ships with increasingly formidable SS-N missiles and later anti-submarine weapons. The first SS-N missiles to enter service were the *Scrubber* missiles, followed by various others, most notably the *Shaddock* (SS-N-3) and the *Styx* (SS-N-2). The latter is probably the most famous of all Soviet missiles since it has found service in seventeen different foreign navies and was responsible for the sinking of the Israeli destroyer *Eilat* in 1967. The *Styx* is employed extensively in light fast patrol boats of the *Osa* and *Komar* classes and has a 40km range at subsonic speeds. Its proven effectiveness – four missiles fired at the *Eilat*, four hits – indicate that, despite the smallness of the patrol craft, it carries a very heavy punch and can deny coastal waters to a powerful enemy. The *Shaddock*, on the other hand, is believed to have a 500km range and to be capable of carrying either a nuclear or conventional warhead. These missiles are also carried on certain Soviet submarines though in this case the range is almost certain to be very much smaller. The whole of this first generation of SS-N missiles is now in the process of being replaced by more modern weapons.

Soviet warships, generally speaking, have been built along general-purpose lines, designed to be able to do a variety of tasks. They seem to be universally the same in that they bristle with armament, radar and electronics, and have not specialized in a given role as the Americans did in the case of the *Spruance* class of destroyer. Com-missioned in 1970, these are the largest ships, other than carriers, to carry virtually no anti-aircraft protection. Besides two 5-in guns they are designed around helicopters, and ASROC missiles and torpedo tubes – a sure indication that they are designed specifically for work with task forces and will rely on carrier aircraft for air defence. Whether the Soviets will follow this lead when they acquire a number of carriers remains to

be seen, though one rather suspects this will not prove to be the case.

The first Soviet step towards an integrated air capability at sea came in the shape of the *Moskva* in 1967. This was initially thought to be a commando carrying ship but the presence of the small *Hormone* class of helicopter identified her as being an anti-submarine cruiser. Her heavy array of AS weapons and sensors confirmed this, but in addition *Moskva* and her sister ship, *Leningrad*, are equipped with considerable facilities for A-A warning and defence, EW and for carrying out a command role. Their rear flight deck would enable them to operate a very limited number of VTOL aircraft. The lack of organic air defence has in part been filled by VSTOL aircraft operating from one of the latest additions to the Soviet Navy, the *Kiev*.

The first Soviet aircraft carrier the *Kiev* **photographed in the Mediterranean by an RAF Nimrod of No 203 Squadron.**

Although designated as an anti-submarine cruiser the *Kiev* displaces about 40,000 tons and has a 600 ft angled flight deck; her carrying capacity has been estimated at being about fifty aircraft, equally divided between *Hormones* and VSTOL aircraft. She is exceptional in that, in addition to her aircraft, she carries SS-N missiles and four Gatling guns for air defence as well as SA-N-3 and SA-N-4 missiles. (The latest American carriers do not carry guns and have no SS capability other than their aircraft.) It is believed that the *Kiev* carries an anti-submarine missile system and may be followed by as many as five sister ships. Overall, though she might not be able to compete with the latest American fleet carrier (though possibly with a light carrier), the *Kiev* marks a considerable advance for the Soviet Navy, both in terms of her political and strategic importance. Her considerable troop lifting capabilities and the strength of her surface-to-surface armament, make her a powerful instrument in the event of a Soviet desire to intervene in some area in the future. Her aircraft enable her to provide some form of defensive umbrella for the fleet at sea and are a possible sign that the Americans will not have matters all their own way in the air over the oceans. As such, this must be a point that marks some shift, however small, in the balance of forces at sea.

Until the time that the Soviets have more *Kievs* at sea, however, the Soviet Navy must still rely on land-based aviation with all the difficulties that such an arrangement implies. They have considerable numbers of long-range aircraft and, in the event of war, could use them *en masse*, possibly in regimental strength of forty bombers, against a Western task force. Any lesser strength might in fact prove inadequate in the event of an invasion force or vanguard task force, the invasion element and rear task force being spread over thousands of square miles of ocean during the approach and possessing considerable anti-aircraft and missile defence capabilities. When all these elements are set alongside her capabilities in mine warfare, and the great problems that they pose for the defence, one can see why the Soviet Navy is causing great concern to the Western Allies. While some take a more sanguine view of Soviet naval developments, it is perhaps timely to make the observation that naval exercises such as *Okean* 75 showed that the Soviets have a world-wide capability that has been considerably enhanced by ever improving RAS facilities: overall, it may be safely noted that the Soviet Navy is an ever growing force that has to be reckoned with.